D1204661

Economic Essays in Honor of ALZADA COMSTOCK

"Those having torches will pass them on to others."

Plato, THE REPUBLIC

PUBLICATION

COMMITTEE

Marjorie S. Belcher

Helen F. Demond

Juliet Fisher Kidney

Everett Day Hawkins
Professor of
Economics and Sociology
1935 —

John Lobb
Professor of
Economics and Sociology
1934—

"Those Having Torches..."

Economic Essays in Honor of

ALZADA COMSTOCK

Presented by Her Former Students

Edited by Lucile Tomlinson Wessmann

Mount Holyoke College, South Hadley, Massachusetts

May, 1954

Essay Index Reprint Series

BOOKS FOR LIBRARIES PRESS
FREEPORT, NEW YORK

Reprinted 1968 by arrangement

LIBRARY OF CONGRESS CATALOG CARD NUMBER:
68-57335

PRINTED IN THE UNITED STATES OF AMERICA

ADVENTURE IN ECONOMICS

Many have studied with Alzada Comstock—been inspired by her, worked hard because of her, learned because of her. A gifted teacher who can make even the subject of finance glow with excitement, she has aroused many a questioning mind and then accompanied it through repeated new discoveries.

Who of her students does not remember Miss Comstock, eyes twinkling, one hand pushing her hair back from her forehead, as she stepped up onto the raised platform of the lecture room and launched into a comment on the important news of the morning? Finance, history, and theory became alive and vital when thus related to the happenings of the day. What appeared on the financial pages and what appeared in the political columns were divorced neither from each other nor from the particular subject we happened to be studying.

Whether it was a corporation and its balance sheet, or a country and its national budget, we were not allowed to forget the people behind these institutions, their history, their hopes, and their aspirations. Through finance as well as economic history, we learned about civilizations. It was an invaluable experience which, upon reflection now, seems to me to have been liberal education at its best.

Former students who have distinguished themselves in the field of economics and those whose economic experiences have been confined to the home, alike remember with gratitude the sense of adventure with which we gathered in Alzada Comstock's classes at Mount Holyoke.

JANET BREWSTER MURROW

PREFACE

This book consists of essays and articles written by former students of Professor Alzada Comstock, member of the Department of Economics and Sociology at Mount Holyoke College from 1913 to 1954. Each was prepared for this book as a tribute to a distinguished and influential teacher, upon the occasion of her retirement. It is presented to her with the hope that it will provide a lasting—though far from complete—reflection of forty-odd years of inspired and inspiring guidance.

Most of the essays and articles fall roughly into the category of economic history which, by something less than pure coincidence, has been Professor Comstock's primary field. British, European, and American subjects have been arranged in that order. A further group of articles deal with subjects in other economic fields in which Professor Comstock taught and worked.

Only a limited number of former students can here represent the thousands who have studied with Professor Comstock. Many others might well have contributed notably to this book; it grew, however, as such books necessarily do, within certain definite limitations that made a wider selection impossible. This we regret, for the present occupations of Professor Comstock's students are varied and their interests broad.

The book represents the combined efforts of many persons in addition to the authors. The Publication Committee not only originated the project and arranged to make its achievement possible but also assisted the editor immeasurably in the planning and production of the book. At least a score of additional alumnae assisted either the Publication Committee or the editor.

We were fortunate to have had available the counsel and technical assistance of T. Robert Stumpf, a graphic designer by profession and an instructor at the New York School of Printing. We are greatly indebted to him, and also to Alfred C. Wessmann of the J. F. Tapley Company, binder of this book, who first encouraged us to believe that we *could* publish a book.

Those of us who are responsible for the actual writing of this volume have worked under one particularly disconcerting handicap. That is the knowledge, ever-present in our minds, that we were attempting the impossible; namely, to do as good a job as Professor Comstock herself could have done. It is a tribute to her lasting position in our affections that so many were willing to try.

LUCILE TOMLINSON WESSMANN

TABLE OF CONTENTS

*Amy Hewes**

ALZADA COMSTOCK

The essays in this volume have been planned as a salute to Alzada Comstock by her former students. Their contributions should furnish some of the evidence of her impress on them and on her college. Her span of teaching, which began in 1913, has been a long and active one. In the course of it many hundreds of young women have studied with her, including a number at Barnard and Smith Colleges as well as those at Mount Holyoke. Different ones of them have known her at different stages of her own development and against a background of the country's changing social history. My part, as a colleague in close touch with her career from almost the beginning, is to put the pieces together and to view it in some perspective.

I am sure it will not surprise anyone who knows her to learn that she is New England born. The scene first familiar to her is the country just north of New London, Connecticut, on the banks of the Thames river. One discovers in her many New England characteristics, not the least of which is her unfailing capacity to get quickly to the gist of the matter. She is as much "against sin" as was the minister in Calvin Coolidge's oft-quoted report, but you are more likely to hear her neatly describe an amusing situation, or she may call your attention to some almost hidden beauty which her eyes were quick to note.

Many of her classmates may remember her as the winner of athletic laurels and the writer of lyrics preserved in volumes of

*Miss Hewes is Professor Emeritus of Economics and Sociology. She taught at Mount Holyoke College from 1905 to 1943.

Mount Holyoke poetry. Her associates on the A. A. U. W., on the other hand, see her, pen in hand, writing study pamphlets for their membership or dashing off to Denmark to confer with European members of the Committee on International Relations about the awarding of fellowships, or smoothing the way for American students and travelers in Norway and Sweden. More recently, her neighbors on Silver Street look for her, not on the golf course but in her garden, where they may find her bent over a hoe making good her reputation as the possessor of a green thumb.

Early Years at Mount Holyoke

Looking back, it seems as if the early years were devoted to deliberate exploration of different fields of interest. After graduation, she returned to Mount Holyoke College as assistant in the Department of Philosophy and Psychology. This was followed by a year at the University of Chicago which yielded a published report on the problems of the negro population of Chicago, based on a field study.

The events of the years leading up to the Ph.D. degree from Columbia University in 1921 were spent in alternate study and teaching under conditions which were varied in geography and in the character of the non-academic undertakings carried on during the summers. They included study at Columbia, at the London School of Economics and in libraries on the continent, field investigating and report writing for the Massachusetts Minimum Wage Commission, and carrying a good share of the responsibility for the Health Officers Training Course for service in munitions plants, offered at Mount Holyoke College during World War I. Again, more than twenty years later, the United States Office of Education, in the summer of 1942, sponsored a course in Industrial Supervision for women to be employed in plants manufacturing war materials for World War II. This course was given at Mount Holyoke College and A. C.'s part in this undertaking required weeks of operating a lathe in a factory on a three-shift schedule.

Professional Interests

Two deep professional interests have been followed continually over the years. The first rests on the conviction that the pattern followed by the modern state in getting and spending its revenue is of first importance in determining its economic development and social welfare. For many years A. C. has given the courses in

Public Finance and in Money and Banking at Mount Holyoke. Ever since the 'twenties, when her texts entitled *State Taxation of Personal Incomes* and *Taxation in the Modern State* were published, she has continuously analyzed and commented on problems in these fields in articles in American financial and economic reviews and more recently in *Current History*, of which she has been a contributing editor since 1943. Appointed by the governor of the Commonwealth, she has represented Massachusetts at meetings of the National Tax Association.

Her second marked professional interest is in the field of economic and social history. She has become a specialist in the problems of the British Commonwealth of Nations and for a number of years has reported their developments in the annual volumes of the *New International Year Book*. Her pleasure and resourcefulness in the field of social history has been expressed in unexpected places. One of these was the charming play entitled *Mount Holyoke Milestones*. This twice scored a victory in being successfully substituted for the quadrennial show of faculty clowns demanded by the students. The play presents episodes in earlier generations drawn from the history of their own institution's century of existence. These delighted the students with their wit and humor in the authentic color of bygone days.

A Forward-Looking Mind

In addition to the advantage of being able to interpret economic problems against their historic background, A. C. has stimulated her students and colleagues by her ability to discern early what was becoming a turning point in world affairs. She attended the first meetings of the League of Nations in Geneva in 1920 and was among the few American scholars to visit and report upon the U. S. S. R. during the first decade of its history. The Guggenheim Fellowship which she held in 1926-1927 was mainly devoted to a study of the financial problems of the countries of central Europe. She attended the San Francisco meeting of the United Nations before its name was decided, as correspondent for the *Springfield Republican* and *Current History*.

A thing of great value which many students have learned from her is the ability to write a sentence in lucid English. This is the most deeply hidden of all professional secrets and I doubt whether A. C. is able to reveal it. Possibly it has some connection with her unbroken rule to read no papers which are not handed in on time. Certainly the students (and faculty members) who have written for the *Mount Holyoke College Studies in Economics and Sociology* edited by A. C. have appeared in print only after memorable encounters with the editor. They knew her as a person who customarily provides for others the same measure of freedom which she enjoys herself. It consequently was a surprise to come suddenly upon a point of no compromise, perhaps over a canon of taste involved or a principle held inviolate.

I join the throng who now express wishes for happy days to come with great confidence in their fulfillment. I can report that the future already looks attractive to her. After years of unremitting hard work, there loom the freedom to write without assignment and the license to devote energy to horticultural projects and canine society—without counting the hours and with no twinge of her New England conscience.

W. Mary Breed
London, England

BRITAIN'S SMALL SHOPKEEPERS

Napoleon is reputed to have called the British a nation of shopkeepers, but a visitor to this country today, who sees only the main shopping streets of our cities and large towns, might well think that we have become a nation of shareholders in co-operatives, department stores and multiples.*

Every town centre appears to offer the same pattern of shopping outlets. There is invariably a co-operative store which, though an independent organization, is linked through the co-operative wholesale suppliers with the other co-operative stores throughout the country. There is the department store which, though independent in appearance, is nowadays likely to be but a unit in a group of similar stores under a central administration and with central buying control. There will be a furniture store belonging to one or other of the big furniture combines. The shoe shops are branches of verticles. The men's outfitters are mostly branches of nation-wide chains.

Shop names repeat themselves from town to town with monotonous regularity. Even the small fashion shops, so innocently styled "Mary Brown" or "Audrey Smith," are as likely as not branches of a chain. And, of course, no town is complete without that most valuable import from across the Atlantic—the Woolworth store.

---

*"Multiple" is the British term for retail outlets with more than three or five branches. By usage, it is distinguished from "chain store," which is a term reserved for a very large "multiple," such as Woolworth, in which all the branches are practically identical, carrying identical merchandise.

On closer acquaintance with our countryside, however, the overseas visitor would discover that the small shops of Britain are by no means extinct. Though driven from the central positions by high rents and rates, as well as by the competition of the larger retail units who can undersell them, they are firmly ensconced in the side streets and on the outskirts of the town, where proximity to the customer is an all-important advantage. They can usually be found on the new housing estates where they supply the day-to-day needs of the young housewife with babies to whom a shopping expedition to the town centre is too heavy an undertaking to be indulged in frequently.

In the smaller towns and villages they still hold the more central sites, cheek by jowl with the powerful competitors who have not yet succeeded in ousting them completely from their traditional position in the business life of the place. In remote hamlets a single small independent is still often the only alternative retail outlet to the local branch of the nearest co-operative store. They vary in type from the smallest general merchant of the Scottish Highlands who has converted his front parlour into a shop, looked after by his wife while he works the adjoining croft, to the main store of the nearest town which sells everything from mousetraps to bedroom suites, and probably serves the countryside by means of travelling vans for twenty miles around.

Less apparent but equally important are the hundreds of small traders who own no shops in the accepted sense, but who sell their wares from stalls in the market place, trading in the same two or three markets on successive days. And finally, there are the itinerant pedlars, the "tallymen" or "Scotch drapers," who take their wares to the consumers' own doors and fulfil a useful function in the distribution of consumer goods in isolated districts.

The 1950 Census of Distribution, the first complete statistical picture of retail trade ever to be compiled in this country, reveals that of 531,143 retail establishments in Great Britain, 414,026 had a turnover of less than £10,000 per year, and 161,566—over 25 per cent—had an annual turnover of less than £2,500. The very small shops, those with an annual turnover of under £1,000, represented one-eighth of the total.

These figures could indeed include small branches of chains, since by definition a retail establishment was taken to mean any place from which goods were sold by retail and they also covered the market stalls, cinema kiosks, mail order houses and all types of itinerant traders. A further table throws some light on the extent of integration. Of the 531,143 retail establishments, 376,537 were one-branch independent shops, and only 45,532 had twenty-five branches and over, while the number of department stores (defined as stores with annual sales of £250,000 and over) was only 323. Returns of the main category of trade were distributed almost equally between food and non-food, the latter shops, with which this article is mainly concerned, accounting for 270,825 of the total.

Public Interest in the Small Retailer

It was the reports of the Retail Trade Committee, set up by the Board of Trade in 1941 to examine the wartime problems of the retail trade in non-food goods, that stimulated public interest in the small retailer. Since that date there has been a succession of books, pamphlets, and magazine articles on retail distribution, in most of which a good deal of space is devoted to consideration of the so-called problem of the small trader, and to suggestions offered as to his proper place in the future economy.

By and large he is not popular with economists and sociologists, and still less with the business efficiency experts. His chief offences are that his distribution costs are higher than those of his larger competitors and he has therefore to take a higher average margin of profit; that in order to compete with lower costs he tends to undercut the wage level, often by exploiting his own labour and that of his family; that he frequently offers long credit; and finally that there are too many of his kind. Added to all this is an assumption that the small trader is inefficient, for if he were efficient, it is argued, he would not be small.

By all the laws of economic theory it might be assumed that the small independent shops should have disappeared long ago in a competitive society. Indeed, an eminent economist writing at the end of the last century confidently stated "the small shopkeeper is losing ground daily." Yet the fact remains that the small traders have survived two major wars, and they have so far held their own against the growing competition of multiples and large departmentals, made keener by the development of modern transport facilities.

This is not to say, of course, that the fight has not been hard and the casualty rate high. It is stated in 1938 over 40 per cent of bankruptcies and receiving orders related to non-food retail traders; the majority would almost certainly have been small traders whose failures could be attributed to inadequate resources and insufficient knowledge of their market. A survey of non-food shops in Leeds covering the first two years of the war showed that 32 per cent of the total number of small single branch shops had already closed due to wartime conditions (shortages, bombing, loss of manpower), as against only 13 per cent of the large shops.

Early Days of the War

Public opinion in this country is easily aroused on behalf of the weaker contestant in a struggle and it was sentiment, rather than a calculated appreciation of the small trader's importance in the scheme of distribution, that inspired the concern for his survival expressed in Parliament in the early days of the war. This led to a policy which, though based on the overriding considerations of public welfare and the furtherance of the war effort, in practice shielded him from the full blast of adverse conditions. To what extent the small shops would have survived without that protection it is impossible to say, but there is little doubt that, had the retail trade been as little controlled as in the 1914-1918 war, the rate of casualty among this class of retailers would have been much higher than it was, and the distribution of consumer goods very much more uneven.

At the same time the very gloomy view of the small shopkeeper's chances of survival taken by the Retail Trade Committee mentioned above, was somewhat exaggerated, for the Committee overlooked the important consideration that as supplies decreased, the rate of turnover was likely to increase, giving all traders a chance to recoup on the roundabouts what they lost on the swings. Moreover, the withdrawal of labour for war requirements tended to strengthen the competitive position of the small man who depends less on outside labour than do the multiples and large stores.

On the assumption that the rate of mortality among retailers was likely to continue high due to the shortage of goods and labour, the Retail Trade Committee proposed a scheme for the orderly withdrawal of traders, and the "marriage" of weaker with stronger units, analogous to the government policy of concentrating factories in manufacturing industries. The scheme, a voluntary one, was commended in particular to the small independent retailer who, the Committee thought, must be asking himself: "What are my prospects? What am I to do?" The withdrawing retailer was to be paid compensation financed by a levy of one per cent on the annual turnover of all retailers remaining in the business, with special provisions for the very small man who was to be given optional exemption.

The scheme was never implemented, due to the opposition of the retailers themselves. The small retailers feared that if they gave up even for the duration of the war, they might never regain their position, and the larger units, who were confident of riding the storm, objected to paying for the casualties in the ranks of the small traders.

In the autumn of 1942 the government formally abandoned its scheme for controlled withdrawal, although it maintained from 1943 to 1945 a voluntary register of withdrawing traders who were guaranteed protective treatment if they wished to re-enter at the close of the war. It also continued and strengthened the measures for controlling entry into the retail trade which had been introduced following the first Report of the Retail Trade Committee. The Location of Retail Business Order of 1941 prohibited entry into retail trade in almost all lines except food, unless under license which was only given when there was a clear case of public need for additional shopping facilities, and furthermore prohibited retailers from pushing out into lines in which they had not formerly dealt. Entry into the food trades was already effectively controlled by the Ministry of Food who, as sole importer of all foodstuffs, and first purchaser of much that was home-produced, had a closer hold on the retailers than ever the Board of Trade had on the distribution of consumer goods.

Restriction of entry, while applicable to all, helped the small trader in particular by the protection it afforded him against competition. The object of the Order, be it said, was to conserve resources for the war effort, but this was usually ignored by retailers who regarded it as a weapon against "unfair" competition (competition is invariably "unfair" to those feeling it), and were the first to insist on its effective enforcement. There is little doubt that in a free market the chains and co-operatives would have pushed out into fresh fields so far as supplies permitted, and the small trader would have been squeezed very hard indeed.

The Fair Shares Scheme

The line of policy pursued by the government from 1942 onwards was aimed at securing fair treatment for all, and afforded some protection to the smaller shopkeepers. Mr. Hugh Dalton, then President of the Board of Trade, said in the House of Commons on 13th October, 1942, "There is a real danger that a large number of the smaller shops may be squeezed out of business. For many reasons that is undesirable. I have therefore come to the conclusion that some positive action is needed to assure to the small retailer his fair share of available supplies."

This action took the form of a scheme whereby a retailer whose annual turnover was under a certain amount could claim from his suppliers a percentage of his purchases made during a standard period before restrictions in production had begun to cause shortages. A tentative attempt was made to cope with the problems of unequal distribution due to the shifts in population during the war by varying the percentages according to areas. The scheme was administered by committees of traders at manufacturing, wholesale and retail levels.

What practical value it had was doubtful. There was nothing in the scheme to prevent a disgruntled supplier from fulfilling his obligations by delivering goods which he knew to be unsuitable to his customer's trade. On the other hand, the public-spirited supplier hardly needed a direction from the Committee to make good some hardship, but if, as quite often proved to be the case, the neglected retailer turned out to be a bad payer or a disagreeable customer, he might have got his due share then, but would have suffered later when supplies ran short. The main weakness of the scheme lay in the fact that goods were getting progressively shorter and soon there were not enough for suppliers to fulfil their obligations, whatever the Fair Shares Committee might decree.

The real value of the Fair Shares Scheme lay in its recognition of the right of the small trader to a fair share of such supplies as were going, and producers and wholesalers were for the most part sufficiently public-spirited to spread the meagre supplies fairly between large and small. Some of the large firms went to enormous trouble in working out their distribution and despatching tiny parcels to their small customers even when the value hardly justified the distribution costs.

It would be unfair to British traders to suggest that the small shopkeepers would have been neglected had the government not exercised its influence on their behalf. For one thing, every supplier wanted to retain such goodwill as he could, knowing that the days of competition would ultimately return. At the same time the temptation to save distribution costs by sending the little there was to the nearest large outlet was strong, and the fact that the government deprecated such action as unsocial undoubtedly had some influence.

Later War Years

As the war progressed and the full effects of the severe cutbacks in production were felt, it became apparent that schemes of distribution based on any standard period of purchases were useless. Moreover, statistical enquiries at consumer level and into retailers' stocks revealed grave inequalities in the distribution of non-food goods between districts. The government, whose first responsibility was to see that the population as a whole was adequately clothed and fed and public morale sustained, resorted to a policy of directing essential goods to places where supplies were judged to have fallen below a critical level, either due to an influx of population, bombing, or any other cause inherent in the wartime conditions. Although at this stage official nursing of the small retailers had to be abandoned, they were still carefully given a generous share in any special distributions, provided they seemed sufficiently efficient to sell the goods in a fair and orderly manner.

Aside from direct government help, the small retailers during the war were directly protected by controls and restrictions which hurt them less than their larger competitors. Mention has already been made of the advantageous position in which they were placed by the withdrawal of employed labour and the rise in wages, conditions which embarrassed a large unit far more than a small one. Petrol restrictions, transport difficulties, and less leisure for shopping drove customers to the little shop that was near. Shortages and standardization of production in clothing and many other lines of goods deprived the larger shops and chains of much of the advantage they ordinarily have to offer in the matter of a wider selection of commodities. Price control had the effect of eliminating competition, so there was little difference in the prices of many goods wherever they were bought and, moreover, the permitted margins were fixed at levels that were considered fair for the small trader even though larger units could probably have operated on a smaller mark-up.

The war then, which at first had seemed to spell doom and disaster for the small shopkeepers, proved a blessing to many of them. Of course there were casualties. In the absence of any census of distribution earlier than 1950, it is impossible to say how many went to the wall, but it seems likely that the mortality rate declined after the first year of the war. It would have been heaviest in the evacuated coastal areas which were denuded of a shopping population. On the other hand, compensating for these closures, licences were issued for 17,849 new shops for which there was a *prima facie* case of consumer need, mostly in districts where demand had increased, and 17,428 of these were for independents.

Dispensable—Or Indispensable?

What of the future? The last control on the retail trade in non-food goods was lifted last year, and this year will probably see the end of food rationing. The retail market is once more theoretically free. What are the prospects of the small retailer now that the protective umbrella of government regulations is withdrawn? Was Professor Alfred Marshall correct in thinking that as the retail trades developed new techniques of distribution, the small retailer would ultimately be squeezed out of existence? Or is he, as described by one of the members of the Retail Trade Committee, a "valuable element and indispensable unit in the economic and social life of the country"?

Time only will provide the final answer to these questions. In the opinion of the writer the small retailer will continue to hold his own so long as he is able to exploit the advantages he still possesses—proximity to his customers and an intimate knowledge of their needs and requirements. His strongest asset is the personal service which he can offer in a higher degree than is possible to his large scale competitors.

Sources:

Retail Trade Committee (Board of Trade): *Report on the opening of New Shops,* H.M.S.O., London, 1941; *Second Interim Report,* 1942; *Third Report,* 1942.

Board of Trade: *Census of Distribution and Other Services,* 1950, *Retail Trade, Short Report,* H.M.S.O., London, 1952.

F. L. Hargreaves and M. M. Gowing: *Civil Industry and Trade,* H.M.S.O., and Longmans Green & Co., London, 1952.

Hermann Levy: *The Shops of Britain,* Kegan Paul, London, 1947.

Henry Smith: *Retail Distribution,* Second Edition, Oxford University Press, London, 1948.

Marion Hamilton Gillim

FAMILY ALLOWANCES IN GREAT BRITAIN

Great Britain has paid cash allowances to families with children since 1946 without regard to income or economic productivity. The Family Allowances Act was passed in 1945 under the Coalition Government, and the amount of the allowances was increased in 1952 under the Conservative Government.

Government payments to subsidize the maintenance of children are not unusual; more than 30 countries have some system of family allowances. Such a program, however, is conspicuous as a departure from British economic tradition, including nineteenth century economic theory, the poor law, and even contributory social insurance. The program involves a redistribution of national income in favor of families with more than one child.

Advocates of Allowances

Family allowances, by the 1920's, had become a cause backed by an enthusiastic and heterogeneous group often possessed with conflicting motives: belligerent feminists and those who sought to keep women at home; religious and left-wing groups; those wanting population growth and some eugenists who hoped the allowances would increase the birth rate among "superior" groups inclined to restrict the size of their families; persons sentimental about children, motherhood and the family, and serious students of child health and welfare; some employers seeking a justification for wages below the level required to support a family and economists concerned with the inadequacy of wages; these, and more, saw family allowances as favoring their particular interests. Organized labor, however, which represented the group expected to benefit most, was slow to accept the plan.

Eleanor Rathbone was the most persistent advocate of family allowances. She wrote "The Remuneration of Women's Services," for *The Economic Journal* in March, 1917, and continued to work for allowances for children throughout her career as Justice of the Peace for Lancashire, President of the feminist National Union of Societies for Equal Citizenship, and as a member of Parliament from 1929 until her death in 1946. She had a sympathetic audience from the start, since the payments to servicemen's families during the war had accustomed many persons to the practice, and the adoption of family allowances on the continent had stimulated public interest.

Her book, *The Disinherited Family,* was so widely read that it had two printings in its year of publication, 1924. In it she criticized economists for presenting theories of distribution which omitted the family as an institution with its own claim on the national income, independent of the occupational contribution of the father. She wrote:

> The subsistence theory of wages was superseded by theories in which wives and children appear only occasionally, together with butchers' meat and alcohol and tobacco, as part of the "comforts and decencies" which make up the British workman's standard of life and enable him to stand out against the lowering of his wages. I do not think it would be an exaggeration to say that, if the population of Great Britain consisted entirely of adult self-propagating bachelors and spinsters, nearly the whole output of writers on economic theory during the past fifty years might remain as it was written . . . .

Miss Rathbone, in her speeches and writings, appeared able to show that family allowances would help to alleviate a wide variety of society's ills. In a biography of Eleanor Rathbone, her friend and co-worker in the Family Endowment Society, Mary Stocks, describes the coverage which Miss Rathbone gave the subject:

> Family allowances . . . could be approached from . . . many directions with . . . infinite variety of emphasis and application. It could be handled as a problem of vital statistics, housing administration, minimum wage legislation, child nutrition, national insurance, teachers' salary scales, coal-mining economics, feminism, social philosophy or pure finance. This is perhaps one reason why Eleanor's handling of it never became, as far as her audiences were concerned, tedious by repetition.

The Disinherited Family emphasized two problems: the inadequate income of the large family and lower pay for women than men in equal work. Miss Rathbone criticized the widely accepted goal of a "living wage" for a "standard family" as being poorly defined, non-existent and impracticable. She argued that a wage large enough to support a family of five would not prevent the suffering of children in larger families and would give to persons with fewer dependents a surplus greater than the economy could afford. She offered family allowances as the solution which would provide for dependents, allow women to receive equal pay with men, and thereby reduce men's fear of wage competition with women.

The persuasiveness of Miss Rathbone's book is shown by its effect on Lord Beveridge who was asked to review it in 1924. In an "Epilogue" to a recent edition of the book he has written: "Till that time . . . I had been apt to regard her and her Family Endowment Society as slightly tiresome creatures, with a particularly loud bee in each of their bonnets . . . . My conversion was immediate and total." He added to the prestige of the movement when, in 1926, as Director of the London School of Economics, he participated in establishing a system of children's allowances for the families of the faculty.

The scope of this article does not permit an analysis of the copious literature of the period on family allowances. Mention must be made, however, of Paul H. Douglas' *Wages and the Family* (Chicago, 1925) in which he presented a plan, designed for conditions in the United States at that time, of family allowances paid from funds contributed by groups of employers. Perhaps the most powerful writing against family allowances was *Family Endowment, A Critical Analysis* (London, 1927) by Alexander Gray. Professor Gray objected to distributing national income on the basis of need and expressed the strong doubt that Miss Rathbone's plan would improve women's position in the economy.

Attitudes of Organized Labor

Organized labor was not convinced that cash family allowances would be in its best interest. There was fear among some trade unionists that the subsidies would weaken collective bargaining and that some employers would find family allowances an excuse for paying lower wages. In 1930 the Joint Committee on the Living Wage of the Labor Party and the Trades Union Congress made a majority report favoring cash family allowances and, also, a minority report recommending, instead, an extension of social services in kind for children. The realization of a program of family allowances was set back when the General Council of the Trades Union Congress, in 1930, adopted the minority report against family allowances. It was twelve years later, in 1942, that the Trades Union Congress decided in favor of family allowances.

The Beveridge Report

In the same year, the authoritative and influential Beveridge Report was published. The Report arose from a survey of social insurance by the Inter-Departmental Committee on Social Insurance and Allied Services of which Lord (then Sir William) Beveridge was chairman. It had been agreed in advance that the report would be prepared and signed by Beveridge alone, since the civil servants representing the various government departments on the committee ought not to be involved in making policy.

The Report listed children's allowances along with health services and the maintenance of a high level of employment as essential to a social insurance system which would eliminate want and, at the same time, preserve the incentive to work. Beveridge estimated that between one-sixth and one-fourth of economic want was ". . . due to the failure to relate income during earning to the size of the family." He believed that family allowances could relieve this want.

He reasoned, also, that the successful operation of unemployment or disability insurance presupposes a system of children's allowances so that benefits may be well below earnings. Social insurance must guarantee during unemployment or disability an income proportional to the number of dependents, even though wages during employment are not related to the size of the family. There was the danger, therefore, that unemployment or disability benefits including payments for children might not be enough below wages to preserve the incentive to seek work. Beveridge recommended that family allowances be paid to both employed and unemployed in order that unemployment and disability benefits would not have to include payments for children and, thus, could be held below wages without causing hardship to children.

Beveridge assumed that wages would cover the cost of two adults and a child. He recommended that an average of eight shillings a week be paid for each child after the first, except, if the parent were unemployed, an additional allowance should be paid for the first child also. The allowances were to be graduated with the age of the child, so that older children would receive larger allowances. The average amount of eight shillings assumed that services, provided directly to children, such as school lunches and free milk, would be continued. The cash allowances were to be non-contributory and paid by the government.

The Family Allowances Bill

The Government's Family Allowances Bill presented to Parliament early in 1945 followed closely the plan outlined in the Beveridge Report. The main point of difference was the setting of the allowance at a flat rate of five shillings per week for each child after the first instead of an average of eight shillings to vary with the age of the child. The lower rate was justified by plans for greater direct services to children, and the flat amount was defended as being more easily administered than one progressing with the age of the child.

The debate on the bill demonstrated that the principle of family allowances had achieved wide acceptance. The chief points of controversy were not whether there should be allowances, but whether the allowance should be granted to the father, as the bill provided, and whether the sum might not be increased. Debate was lively on the greater reliability of the mother than the father to see that the child would benefit from the spending of the allowance. Eleanor Rathbone participated in the debate to support a measure which she had promoted for more than 20 years and to argue at length that the mother and not the father should receive the allowance.

The Family Allowances Bill became law on June 15, 1945. It had been amended to provide that the allowance should belong to the mother, but the amount of the subsidy was left at five shillings. Payment of the allowances began in August, 1946.

The rapid rise in the cost of living following the start of the Korean War strengthened the demand for increased allowances. The Family Allowances and National Insurance Act of 1952 amended the original act by providing that the allowances be increased from five to eight shillings per week. The increased rate began in September, 1952.

How the Program Works

Since 1952 every family with more than one child has been eligible to receive a weekly cash allowance paid by the government with no previous contribution by the family. A child qualifies until he reaches the school-leaving age (usually fifteen years) or until the first of August after his sixteenth birthday if he is a full-time student or an apprentice. The amount of the allowance is eight shillings per week for each child except the first below the specified age. The program is supervised by the Ministry of Pensions and National Insurance which issues books of stamps to be cashed weekly at the local post office.

The survey by the Ministry of Labor and National Service for April, 1953, showed the average weekly earnings of a man in manual work to be 186 shillings. The allowance to a family with two children would be equivalent to a bonus of four per cent of the average worker's earnings, and for a family with six children to a bonus of over 20 per cent. The allowance would be even more important to the many families with earnings below the average.

The *Fourth Report of the Ministry of National Insurance* shows that, at the end of 1952, allowances were being paid for 4.8 million children to over 3 million families who had 8 million children below the age limit. Almost two-thirds of the families with allowances had only two children and, therefore, an allowance for only one child. More than one-fourth of the population belonged to families receiving the allowances. The annual cost to the government for 1953-54 was expected to be £104 million.

Cash Allowances and Tax Exemptions

Besides a system of cash family allowances, the United Kingdom has provisions for children's exemptions in the determination of taxable income for the income tax. The payment of cash allowances requires the elaborate machinery of stamp books and the awarding and subsequent taxing back of unnecessary cash allowances to families with large incomes. The income tax exemptions, on the other hand, are relatively easy to administer, but they were criticized for granting allowances only to families with incomes high enough to tax.

Many suggestions have been made for avoiding this double granting of family allowances in both cash payments and income tax exemptions. These proposals have ranged from a plan to eliminate the income tax relief in respect of children and to use the increased revenue for augmenting the amount of the cash allowances, to a plan to restrict cash allowances to families with income too low to get an equivalent allowance under the income tax. The latter proposal was examined in a White Paper on *Family Allowances* in 1942 (Cmd. 6354). The scheme would have given parents the choice between the children's exemption under the income tax and the cash payment.

The White Paper pointed out that the combining of the two types of allowances might postpone the reduction of income taxes by increasing the government's tax loss corresponding to any given tax reduction. It was argued that a decrease in the tax burden would reduce the value of the exemption to the taxpayer and result in more requests for the cash allowances. The White Paper concluded, as did the Beveridge Report some months later, that the two kinds of allowances have different aims and that no attempt should be made to substitute cash allowances for tax rebates.

From the point of view of compensatory fiscal policy, however, the treating of cash allowances and income tax exemptions as alternatives could increase the flexibility inherent in a progressive income tax. In a business recession, a decline in taxable incomes would automatically be accompanied not only by lower effective tax rates, but also by increased payments in cash subsidies. Conversely, rising taxable incomes would be taxed at higher rates and the payments in cash allowances would decline as the use of tax exemptions increased. The inequity of the plan lies in the fact that both the benefits and hardships resulting from the added flexibility fall more heavily on taxpayers with children.

Although their aims may be different, the cash allowances and tax exemptions are linked by the tax. In the tax year 1953-1954, an exemption from taxable income of £85 for each child is allowed for the calculation of the income tax (but not for the surtax). The rate progresses in the lower incomes through three brackets from 12½ per cent to a proportional rate of 45 per cent on taxable income above £400 per year. The result is a tax saving which increases with income until, at the maximum rate of 45 per cent, the tax is reduced by £38 5s. for each child. For example, the maximum exemption is reached for a family with two children at an earned income slightly above £1,000 per year.

The cash allowances are subject to the income tax and, when net income exceeds £2,000 per year, to the progressive surtax. The combined income tax and surtax rates, ranging from 12½ per cent of the lowest taxable income to 95 per cent of net income over £15,000 per year, reduce the amount of the cash family allowances remaining after tax as family income increases. The value to be retained by the family from the cash allowances declines from £20.8 per year for each eligible child after the first in families without taxable income to £1 per year in families with incomes above £15,000.

The adding of the cash allowance and the tax savings from the children's exemption gives a total family allowance which rises with income, reaches a plateau, and then declines through the higher income ranges. The combined value of the tax saving and the cash allowance after tax is at a maximum in a family of two children, for example, at an annual income between £1,000 and £2,000—where the "value" of the second child is about £50.

Indeterminate Effects

Since allowances are not large enough to make children profitable and are relatively unimportant among the forces affecting wages, the aggregate effects of the payments are not readily determined. The remarkable thing is not the effects or lack of effects to be observed from the allowances, but rather the quiet acceptance of the principle. *The Economist* said on February 24, 1945: "Once the principle of family allowances is accepted and embodied in a statute, succeeding Parliaments will always be able to press for an amending measure to increase the amount."

Selected Bibliography

Douglas, Paul H.: *Wages and the Family,* 2nd edition, University of Chicago Press, 1927.

Gray, Alexander: *Family Endowment: A Critical Analysis.* Benn, London, 1927.

Great Britain, British Information Services: *Social Services in Britain,* revised, 1953.

Great Britain, Chancellor of the Exchequer: *Family Allowances.* Cmd. 6354 H.M.S.O., London, 1942.

————: *Financial Statement,* 1953-54. H.M.S.O., London, 1953.

Great Britain, Ministry of National Insurance: *Reports* H.M.S.O., London.

Great Britain: *Social Insurance and Allied Services,* Beveridge Report, Cmd. 6404, H.M.S.O., London, 1942.

Rathbone, Eleanor: *Family Allowances,* new ed. of *The Disinherited Family,* Allen & Unwin, London, 1949.

Stocks, Mary D.: *Eleanor Rathbone: A Biography,* Gollancz, London, 1949.

United Nations, Department of Social Affairs: *Economic Measures in Favour of the Family,* New York, 1952.

Rosemary Danes Hale

BRITAIN'S TRADE 1945 - 1950: AN EXAMPLE OF SOCIALIST PLANNING

During the first five postwar years Britain's international trade was planned as one part of an overall program. This study examines the following questions:

Why did Britain plan?
How was trade organized?
What was the trade policy?
Did controls mushroom?

Regulation of international trade, however, dates back to 1931 when the United Kingdom departed from its traditional free trade policy. It enacted protective tariffs insulating domestic agriculture from foreign competition and established a system of imperial preference. At the start of World War II, Britain's international trade was subjected to financial and commercial controls designed to further "economic warfare." At the same time, rigid controls were imposed upon the internal economy of the United Kingdom. Britain's abandonment of free trade and its adoption of direct controls during the war were approved by both major political parties.

In 1945, the Labour Party came into power in Great Britain with an election mandate (or so the party interpreted it) partially to socialize the nation. In their five years of power, the Labourites did not adopt the "centralized scheme" or overall planning of the type practiced by the U.S.S.R. Neither did they attempt the "competitive solution" which has been propounded as a means of allocating resources under a socialist regime. Instead, piece-meal and partial planning were adopted.

The answer to the question "why did Britain plan?" was never given precisely. The most exact definition was the one given in the *Economic Survey* for 1947 which stated: "The object of economic planning is to use the national resources in the best interests of the nation as a whole." A perusal of this and subsequent surveys leads one to the conclusion that the British planners did not see a need to define their goal in more specific terms. In addition, there seemed to be little interest in or understanding of the central problem of resource allocation. Despite this apparent unconcern with fundamentals, there was agreement that division of the national product among the major claimants should be made by the government.

Although a precise goal was never announced, scattered throughout the official literature one finds various reasons for planning. Among the most oft-repeated are that Britain planned to secure full-employment, to attain a higher standard of living, to solve the dollar and other balance-of-payments problems, to secure "fair shares," to achieve economic independence, to make possible capital reconstruction and development, and to provide an adequate military defense.

Piece-Meal Controls

For the whole economy British socialists favored a policy of piece-meal rather than comprehensive controls. Among the controls imposed were regulation of capital investment, rationing of foodstuffs and clothing to consumers and of raw materials to industry, price controls, guaranteed agricultural prices, rent ceilings, and direction of land utilization. Controls were inter-related; no one measure could be considered the sole regulator and private initiative retained a residual role. Prominent also among the control instruments were the indirect levers of government expenditure, taxation, and fiscal policy, which are not exclusively socialist tools. There was strong support for a gradual shift from direct, piece-meal methods to the indirect mechanism of monetary and fiscal regulators, but British planning relied on a mixture of methods during the period.

It was stated in the *Economic Surveys* that government's role was to define and delineate the "national task" or working pattern. Plans originated in a central staff, working with government departments, which assessed the national resources and formulated the needs of the economy. Next, a series of economic budgets was drawn up which related the needs to the resources, thereby indicating the most efficient use of the available factors of production. The third step was to devise control methods which permitted the budgets to be attained "without interfering with democratic freedoms." In addition, there were analyses of particular problems. This combination of programs, sometimes expressed in monetary units and at other times in terms of manpower, indicated priorities among the most essential tasks. But it did not exhaustively catalogue resources, specifically allocating each unit to a particular use as in the Russian Five-Year Plans.

Plans were often changed, frequently before they had been completed. As the *Economic Surveys* devoted so much space to justifying the flexibility of British planning, it is well to catalogue the most often repeated justifications for the apparent contradiction of laying down annual plans or goals which were not necessarily binding. First, it was stressed that British planning was democratic and dependent in the last analysis upon individual voluntary cooperation; everyone must therefore understand the objectives and be consulted concerning their attainment either before or after the goals were set. The precise time of consultation was not uniform.

Second, plans were short-term in character; for dependence on international trade, it was urged, made only short-term planning practical. Flexibility was stressed as necessary in view of the international competition Britain must meet. Third, plans were changed to provide the maximum selection of goods and to assure the most varied production pattern; the complexity of Britain's economy made it inadvisable to plan precisely. This last admission, if true, obviously limits the utility of planning as a method for acquiring a higher standard of living, except perhaps in primitive countries.

Import and Export Goals

The annual economic blueprint laid down total import and export goals by commodity, source and destination. Import goals could be reasonably exact, for British purchases were mainly primary products used to produce manufactured goods or to feed the population, and regulation of such consumption was within the government's power. Export problems were considerably more complicated. Pin-point accuracy was neither hoped for nor expected, as it was explained that willingness of foreign customers to buy and of their governments to allow such purchases was beyond the control of British planners.

Overall regulation of commodity trade was vested in the Board of Trade which licensed both imports and exports with the exception of the sterling area trade, which was free. An inter-governmental committee supervised the trade program. The issuing of a permit by the Board of Trade (or in the case of certain specific products by other agencies), authorized the sale or purchase of specific goods from particular sources or to named consignees. In addition, there were semi-official groups which tackled particular export problems, such as the "Dollar Export Board."

Exports were generally handled by private traders. Imports, on the other hand, were procured in two different ways. Some were bought in bulk by government departments directly from foreign sellers. Others were imported by private firms on an historical quota basis. Government purchases appeared to be confined to "essential" raw materials and foodstuffs while private traders procured other types. According to monopoly theory, such buying power should have placed the British government in a strong position to strike advantageous bargains. British critics, however, complained bitterly that the combination of a post-war seller's market and inefficiency within the purchasing departments dissipated this power.

Every attempt was made to reduce imports to the irreducible minimum necessary to feed and clothe Britons. Imports, however, were needed for the production of manufactured exports. And exports were encouraged even at the expense of the domestic consumer. A variety of devices were used to direct goods toward the export market. Domestic competition for exportable goods was restricted by rationing, re-enforced by price control and further reduced by the imposition of purchase taxes ranging from 16-2/3 to 100 per cent. Imports were controlled to balance Britain's foreign accounts and to reduce foreign borrowing. In addition, taxation, the rationing of foodstuffs, and the allocation of raw materials (with considerable weight given to successful exportation) were devices used to limit imports by volume.

Dollar Gap Problems

British planning efforts to eliminate the balance of payments problem went beyond the fostering of exports and the reduction of imports. Of paramount importance were the problems of directing exports to particular markets and the procuring of imports from purchasers of British goods. This was the crux of the much publicized "dollar problem" or "dollar gap."

The export goal was more difficult to attain, particularly as little was done to force exporters to invade the American hard currency market. Targets were set in the *Economic Survey* for total sales to particular currency areas. But as late as May 1949 no attempt was made to make one more attractive than another except indirectly by allocating raw materials, allowing British sellers to spend dollars to advertise their wares, carrying on and encouraging market research, and making available the facilities of the Export Credit Guarantee Department.

Indirectly, the problem was attacked by promoting exports to the sterling area, thereby reducing the demand of those countries for identical dollar imports and hence husbanding the dollar reserve of the area. Exports to "soft currency" countries were limited if the goods were badly needed at home. Presumably the converse was true in relation to the acquisition of "hard currency." At times exports were classed as non-essential by foreign planners who refused to allow such British goods into their markets. And the picture was further complicated by the scarcity of all goods in Britain's home market, making it politically inexpedient for the planners to allow many "unrequited exports"—those which were not exchanged for imports.

Reduction of imports, especially those from the dollar area, posed other problems. As far as possible, British buyers and other sterling area purchasers were diverted from the hard currency area. Domestically produced goods were substituted for imports by expanding home production. Compensation for some reductions was achieved by creating new import sources in nations with which Britain had an export balance or political and economic ties.

Such innovations were not without their drawbacks. At times the new source was high-cost in comparison to the old supplier, and British exports manufactured with these materials were priced out of the market. Another serious obstacle arose frequently when suppliers of "essential" imports tied their sales to less necessary goods which the British did not desire.

In the matter of trade policy British planners paid lip-service to multilateralism by fostering the International Trade Organization, joining the twin Bretton Woods agencies, and working within the Organization for European Economic Cooperation for limited European convertibility. At the same time, however, Britain was a party to numerous bilateral trade agreements, sterling convertibility was extremely limited, and every effort was made to balance accounts with each currency area.

Conclusion

From the point of view of economic theory, the program followed by the British was less effective in allocating resources and maximizing satisfactions than the alternatives available. Even centralized Russian-type planning would probably have achieved better results. Certainly there is every indication that a competitive free market system upon either a socialist or capitalist base would have been more effective in raising living standards. As a practical matter, however, Britain's flexibility had the advantage of alteration in the light of experience. It should also be borne in mind that the Labour Party had interests other than raising the standard of living. Actually, it was more concerned with the equalization of real income (or at least the eradication of income extremes).

Direct controls have frequently been described as a definitive departure or a "point of no return." Such restrictions have been proclaimed by both friend and foe to mushroom and to be permanent. British experience with flexible, piece-meal planning does not substantiate these conclusions. The controls remained selective and their scope was unchanged. Instead of increasing, state trading actually declined somewhat as various commodities were returned to the hands of private traders.

Finally, it will never be possible to prove that Britain's experiment in socialist control of international trade was either a success or a failure. Such proof could only be obtained were it possible to have Britain re-experience the years 1945-1950 under a system of free multilateral trade. Since the hands of the clock cannot thus be turned back, we can only surmise the results of such an experiment.

Sources:

Information herein contained was taken from the official *Economic Surveys* of 1947, 1948, 1949 and 1950 (H.M.S.O., London), Cmd. 7046, Cmd. 7344, Cmd. 7647, Cmd. 7915 and Cmd. 7572; current British periodicals, particularly *The Economist, Midland Bank Review, Lloyds Bank Review* and *The Economic Journal; Labour and Industry in Britain, Board of Trade Journal* and other government documents; and writings of prominent British socialists.

*Elinor Harris**

PROBLEMS OF FRENCH TAX REFORM

One of the most troublesome chronic issues in France has been the reform of the French tax system. Financial experts are agreed upon the urgent desirability of such a reform. Nevertheless, the weakness of French governments and the strength of farmers, retail traders, and other groups who are "protected" under the present tax regime, present powerful and apparently insuperable barriers to any fundamental tax revision.

Contrary to popular belief in this country, the French pay very heavy taxes relative to their incomes. While the per-capita gross national product in France is only one-third as great as in the United States, the overall fiscal burden (including contributions to social benefits) represents a somewhat greater proportion of the gross national product in France than in this country. However, this heavy burden is distributed inequitably among occupational groups and income classes; French farmers, artisans, and small shopkeepers are able to evade taxes to a considerable extent, while wage-earners and large corporations are far less able to do so.

The French fiscal system is noted also for complexity, for the numerous duplications of tax levies, and for inflexibility. An additional problem is the great preponderance in the French tax structure of sales and other indirect taxes; these tend to dampen investment incentives through increasing the cost of private in-

*The author is an economist with the Division of International Finance of the Board of Governors of the Federal Reserve System. The opinions expressed are her personal views and must not be construed as representing the views of the Board of Governors.

vestment financing, and to impair the French competitive position through raising production costs and prices of the finished product.

Aggregate Tax Burden a Heavy One

Aggregate figures, as shown in the French national accounts, indicate that the French tax structure as a whole yields substantial revenue. For instance, in 1952 tax revenues of all French government units amounted to 4,200 billion francs ($12 billion at the official rate of exchange), or about 32 per cent of gross national product. In contrast, our Federal, state, and local tax revenues in 1953, totaling $92 billion, represented only about 27 per cent of gross national product. However, if revenues used to finance welfare and other social costs—an unusually heavy item in the French budget—were excluded from the measure in both countries, the fiscal burden in France and the United States would be more nearly equal, being reduced to about 21 per cent of the French and about 23 per cent of the U. S. gross national product.

Payments from government to private citizens for social welfare, retirement and other purposes are relatively higher in France than in the United States, chiefly because of great differences in economic structure and social institutions in the two countries. For one thing, wages and salaries are a relatively smaller proportion of the French than of the U. S. national income, as a result of the controlled wage levels in France and the vast numbers of farmers, small shopkeepers, and other "middlemen."[1] For another thing, substantial retirement and other social benefits in the United States are paid for privately from private insurance and voluntary industrial pension funds, a practice less common in France.

Similarly, net subsidies and direct payments to government enterprises play a negligible role in the U. S. budget, but amounted in 1952 to 14 per cent of government expenditures in France. A

[1]Wages and salaries in 1952 formed only 56 per cent of the national income in France in contrast to 66 per cent in the United States; property and entrepreneurial income were a correspondingly larger part of the national income in France than in the United States, mainly because of the greater predominance in France of retailers and other types of "middlemen." On the other hand, consumers' expenditures on goods and services represented 69 per cent of GNP in France, as compared with only 62 per cent in the United States; gross private investment and government expenditure on goods and services were each smaller fractions of GNP in France than in the United States.

very large French budget item has been expenditure on behalf of the Modernization and Equipment Fund, which helps finance investment requirements of basic French industries including primarily the large nationalized industries (coal, gas, electricity, and railroads). On the other hand, a large part of the U. S. Government aid to business or individuals takes the form of loan guarantees (which become an actual budgetary expenditure only if the loan should fail to be repaid at some future date) or direct lending on the part of long-established government corporations (such as the Rural Electrification Administration). Since these corporations, on balance, earn profits or realize only very small losses, such aid does not appear either as an expenditure of the U. S. Government in the national accounting sense or as a burden to the taxpayer. The developed capital market in the United States also makes possible greater private financing of the investment needs of these Federal corporations as well as of state and municipal government requirements.

Thus it may be concluded that the aggregate tax burden in France is higher than in this country mainly because of the more sizable French public welfare and investment programs and the greater degree of nationalization of French industry. The extensive postwar public financing of French investment requirements, in turn, has been necessary because of the lack of adequate private saving and private investment financing. The per-capita gross national product in France is only about one-third as great as in this country, however; even the same percentage burden of taxation would therefore involve much greater hardship on the individual French taxpayer. The burden is further enhanced by the fact that the French tax system, in view of its reliance on indirect taxes, bears more heavily than the U. S. system on the low-income groups and relatively less heavily on the high-income group.[2]

A Regressive Tax Structure

The bulk of French Central Government tax revenues in 1952 (75 per cent) was derived from production, sales, and other indirect taxes, which generally constitute an element of cost and price and are levied irrespective of income level or ability to pay; only a small fraction of U. S. Federal Government revenues (16

---

[2]For a thorough discussion of the French tax system, see Ministère des Finances, *Note Sur le Système Fiscal Français* (Paris, May 1, 1952).

per cent) was derived from such taxes. Moreover, although the share of indirect taxes has lately been decreasing in the United States, it is continuing to increase in France.

Although there is little resemblance in the tax structure of the two countries at the central government level, the tax structure of the French municipalities is very similar to that of U. S. state and local governments. In both cases, there is a heavy dependence upon property, sales, and miscellaneous license taxes, although U. S. state governments make somewhat greater use of direct corporate and personal income taxes. Similarly, both French and U. S. municipalities have been forced in the postwar period to seek new revenue sources, most of them indirect (and therefore regressive) in nature. Receipts from the French property tax (*"centimes additionnels"*), a major but inflexible source of local government revenue, have not kept pace with rising government costs in the postwar years. French municipalities, in general, have found the bulk of new tax resources in new business transactions taxes (*"taxe locale additionnelle aux taxes sur le chiffre d'affaires"*) or increased rates on existing business, license, service, or contract taxes, just as several state governments in our country have turned to new sales taxes.

At the local government level, these particular new tax sources tend to be passed on to the consumer in the form of higher prices. At the central government level, the heavy burden of indirect taxes—intensified by great postwar increases in taxes on business transactions (*"chiffre d'affaires"*)—also must have raised prices of French finished products, particularly in a situation characterized by intense inflationary pressures and strong consumer demand for goods. However, attempts have been made to shift the burden of consumers' taxes somewhat from the lowest-income groups through exempting certain types of necessities and food products from the transactions tax (normally levied at the rate of 1 per cent on all services, imports, and retail sales); a similar procedure has frequently been adopted also by U. S. state governments to reduce the regressive impact of new sales taxes. The French production tax, too, taxes food and other necessities at a lower rate than it does non-essential commodities.

These measures in France—in conjunction with the expanding social budget and the transfer of some of the personal income taxes on wages and salaries to the employer—have probably helped to reduce the heavy fiscal burden upon the low- and middle-income groups; at the same time, the liberal French family allowance system has tended to shift the remaining burden onto the unmarried and childless. In 1952, social security payments were equal to about 30 per cent of total payrolls. Although employees' contributions are largely regressive (i.e., constitute a larger proportion of the income of low than of high-income groups), the net effect of the program as a whole is to make the French fiscal system somewhat more progressive. Employers make the major contribution to its costs, while recipients tend to be in the lower- or middle-income groups.

The rise, between 1938 and 1952, in yields from direct taxes (chiefly personal and corporate income and inheritance taxes) from 17 to 25 per cent of total central government receipts has also tended to make the French fiscal structure somewhat more equitable. To judge from the actual effective rate schedules, the rate structure of the French personal income tax itself would appear to be as steeply progressive as that of the United States in the case of the married man with two children; it must be remembered also that the same man in France would receive a family allowance from the Government. Moreover, according to the published schedules, the French income tax schedule is probably more progressive than ours in the case of a single French wage earner with no dependents.

Inequality Intensified by Widespread Tax Evasion

Nevertheless, in actual practice the French income tax structure is probably less progressive than the American one (that is, bears less heavily upon the upper-income groups) because of the widespread tax evasion in the upper-income brackets. Most medium and large corporations and all wage and salary earners have great difficulty evading tax payments because their incomes are, in general, known to the tax authorities, and actual payments can be closely checked. On the other hand, income taxes on unincorporated business firms, farmers, and the professional classes, who can most easily conceal incomes, are very difficult to identify and to collect.[3] Wide-spread evasion in these cases tends to pro-

[3]See "Le Système Fiscal Français Avant et Après La Reforme," *Notes et Etudes Documentaires,* August 26 and August 27, 1949. These particular "protected" groups who can best evade or escape tax payment play a far more important role in French economic life than they do in the United States, and result in an added element of cost and price; thus in 1951 the farmers, professional classes, and unincorporated business firms produced an estimated 25.5 per cent of the gross national product in France, as compared to only 12.4 per cent in the United States.

tect probably the least efficient economic units—the small artisan and retailer—and, at the same time, to penalize the business corporation, whose efficiency and ability to reduce costs and prices of domestically produced goods appear to be greatest.

Enforcement of business income and transactions taxation at the retail level (including attack on the tendency of the retailer to collect but pocket the tax) was recently tightened, but attempts to obtain new legislation on taxation of agricultural income have been largely unsuccessful. Present taxable land valuations still have been set at only fifteen or twenty times the 1908 values, whereas wholesale agricultural prices have increased by about 170 times over the same period.

Savings and Investment Incentives Damaged

Although postwar public investment financing in France has been fairly large, private expenditure for investment has lagged. Tax policy appears actively to discourage private business investment, although introduction of new techniques would be essential in order to lower the French cost-price structure, improve the standard of living, and strengthen the country's ability to compete abroad and thus her external balance. Fiscal policy does little if anything to encourage corporate and personal savings, although the country is plagued by under-saving; or to encourage the channeling of savings from gold or other hoards into productive investment.

Since French taxes on the whole bear down heavily upon consumption, one might assume that saving was accorded favorable treatment; the relatively heavier burden of taxation upon lower- and middle-income groups (who tend to save relatively less of their incomes) and the lighter burden upon the higher-income groups (who ordinarily tend to save relatively more) would seem to suggest, too, that saving might be stimulated while consumption was penalized. The facts do not appear to bear out this hypothesis, however; saving in a form which can be utilized for investment purposes has been extremely low in postwar France. The Government could best encourage personal and corporate saving by establishing confidence in the maintenance of currency stability through fiscal and monetary policies. Actually, these policies instead have dampened incentives to save because they have failed to avoid periodic inflations, which destroy the value of money savings.

Since 1948, the rise in French gross national product at current monetary values has been the greatest of any country of Western Europe. Even when deflated by a combined consumer and wholesale price index, the increase between 1948 and 1952—about 21 per cent—remains substantial. Such data help support the thesis that individual savings in France have not been retarded primarily by any lack of growth of real incomes but rather by the inflationary bias in the French economy, for which weak tax measures have been at least partly responsible. France's failure to achieve financial and monetary stability has made it impossible for her to achieve any substantial postwar rise in personal inclinations to save (i.e., in the *ratio* of savings to incomes). It has also influenced unfavorably the financial forms in which personal savings are held: given an expectation of more or less permanent inflation, investors were reluctant to hold assets whose money value was fixed, such as savings deposits and ordinary bonds.

High Interest Rates

There is at present, therefore, a strong desire to keep savings in gold, land, or other assets, the value of which will not depreciate with further declines in the purchasing power of the French franc. The interest rate, in France, must not only provide a return upon investment and compensate for the risk of loss on the capital venture itself; it must also cover the risk of capital losses on fixed-interest assets due to a decline in the purchasing power of the currency.

Actually, interest rates, though high enough to retard private investment, have not been high enough to induce sufficient purchases by non-bank investors of government and private bonds; during the past two years it has been necessary, in addition, to link the value of bonds to a commodity of constant purchasing power, such as the gold Napoleon, kilowatt hours of electricity, or railroad passes. Still, as shown by a recent study of French investment preferences, the public's enthusiasm for such "indexed" loans remains slight, and until late 1953 the most popular forms of savings continued to be real estate and gold. However, with the recent decline in gold prices on the French market, buyers' interest in gold as a form of investment has declined and some private dis-hoarding of gold has apparently taken place.

It is somewhat more difficult to explain the lack of investor interest in equities of business corporations, the monetary value of which may well rise with an increase in the price level and the money value of corporate profits. Dividend income in France, as in the United States, is taxed twice—once at the corporate level, and, when profits are distributed to stockholders, at the personal level. It has been alleged that this double taxation tends to discourage the supply of investment funds flowing into business equities. This feature of the tax structure appears less significant in explaining the relatively low demand for equities, however, than do other economic factors and psychological attitudes. These include the low level of corporate dividend payments; the fear of further nationalization of industry; and, finally, the greater familiarity of most individuals with gold hoarding than with stock investment as a hedge against inflation.

Three Facets of the Investment Problem

The problem of reducing the heavy impact of French taxation upon investment seems, first of all, to be dependent upon redistributing more equitably the tax load between corporations and non-corporate enterprise.[4] The tax system is alleged to discriminate against the more efficient, large-scale corporate producer (who cannot feasibly escape payment either of the corporate income tax or the employees' payroll tax) as against the self-employed artisan (who may manage to evade payment of part of the individual income tax or part of the transactions tax).

Second, the operation of the French production tax, levied on each sale or transaction and at each level of production, discriminates against the production of goods the fabrication of which requires many productive stages. Finally, the production tax tends to discriminate against the use of productive capital equipment as against the use of manpower. Business investment expenditures, used to improve production techniques, are penalized to the extent that they are subject to such a tax, while labor costs or raw materials purchases are entirely exempt. In order to alleviate this situation, Finance Minister Faure in late 1953 succeeded in reducing the production tax on business equipment purchases by fifty per cent, a measure expected to result in a ten per cent decline in the cost of investment goods. A reduction in the rediscount rate of the Bank of France from 4 to 3½ per cent was supposed to decrease private bank rates generally and, thereby, similarly reduce investment costs and stimulate private capital outlays.

---

[4]This problem is discussed in the study of the Finance Ministry, "Productivité et Fiscalité," *Statistiques & Financières,* June 1952.

At the same time, the Finance Minister emphasized, as the guiding principle of his policy of "expansion without inflation," that savings out of national income should be increased, too, if total private investment is to rise—a goal not likely to be attained unless internal financial stability can be achieved and sustained.

Even without any substantial increase in tax revenues, strengthened individual savings incentives and a greater willingness on the part of the non-banking public to invest in Government bonds would help to alleviate the chronic French budgetary problem. It is doubtful, however, whether the Government can obtain the required amount of non-inflationary financing out of savings of non-bank investors until it persuades Parliament to approve a genuine tax revision, which would strengthen confidence in the currency and help restore private savings to an adequate level.

Frances C. Manning

THE CRISIS IN FRANCE

The struggle between the forces of liberty and those of totalitarianism has become a clear-cut contest between two opposing coalitions, each attempting to make maximum use of its strength and resources by welding its component nations into a unified whole. Just as the strength of a chain is impaired if an individual link is weak, so is the strength of a coalition reduced by weakness in any of its chief members. The United States, as leader of the free world coalition, is therefore vitally concerned that its associates maintain the economic vigor and psychological fortitude on which depends our success in the conflict with international communism.

More than $40 billion in goods and services have already gone into our effort to bolster our coalition. For the most part, this investment in future peace and security has had gratifying success. Although Western Europe, which shares with Canada and the United States the burden of providing the industrial strength of the free world, has not yet solved all the problems of survival in a sharply divided world, it has at least reached the point where large-scale economic assistance is no longer needed or desired, and where even military assistance is expected to be on a declining scale.

The most important exception to this generally satisfactory situation is France. There, the dynamic recovery of the early postwar years, which had carried French industrial activity to all-time peak levels in 1951 and 1952, appears to have lost its momentum. Production declined significantly during 1953, and foreign exchange problems are once again alarming.

Even more disturbing than these signs of economic weakness, however, is the growing evidence of social and political unrest. Factionalism, which was submerged during the years of concentration on physical reconstruction, has now reappeared in such virulent form as to preclude any hope of stability or unity without drastic and far-reaching reforms in government and social organization. These divisive forces, said Hanson Baldwin in *The New York Times* on December 24, 1953, "are of such long duration and reflect such deep schisms that it probably is fair to say that modern France will not be able to develop her potential greatness and exercise it fully in the political and military fields unless: (a) a virtual political, social and economic revolution occurs; or (b) another Napoleon unifies and uplifts the French people."

The Cornerstone of European Unity

While the difficulties confronting France are primarily matters of internal policy, they have much wider import; in fact, the progress of the free world coalition is dependent on their prompt amelioration. This follows not only because of the importance of France as a major power in the alliance, but also because of her strategic role as the cornerstone of Continental European Unity. Without a strong, resilient France, the difficulties of securing military defense and achieving political harmony and economic cooperation among the Continental nations grow immeasurably greater.

Each major step which still remains to be taken toward European unification leads ultimately to the unresolved question of Franco-German relations. As long as Germany's star is rising, there is little likelihood of satisfactory *rapport* unless France also is negotiating from strength. French fears of a resurgent Germany, intensified by doubts as to her own economic power and internal cohesion, have prolonged the debate over the creation of a European Defense Community and postponed further progress toward that political integration of the Continent which the London *Economist* terms "the only positive political idea that presents itself to European youth."

Why is France the laggard? What special characteristics of her structure are responsible for the present apparent inability to maintain her industrial activity, her political stability, and her international solvency? Certainly, there is no lack of resources. France has more than adequate living space for her population;

her agriculture is well-developed; her mineral resources and industrial raw materials, though limited in quality and variety, are nonetheless extensive; her workers are frugal, industrious and intelligent. Why, with these ingredients for sound economic development and social progress at her disposal, has France failed to realize her potential power?

Reconstruction and Other Burdens

In part, the present situation in France is traceable to the extremely heavy burden she has been carrying in recent years. The devastation of her homes, factories and transport facilities during the war has necessitated huge expenditures on a reconstruction program which is not yet fully completed. German and Italian reparations payments have been negligible and by far the greatest share of this expense has been borne by France herself. Gross domestic investment, which was not more than 10-12 per cent of total national expenditure in prewar years, has been increased to nearly double the former rate.

In addition, France has had to finance the seven-year conflict against Communist forces in Indo-China, which involved a drain of manpower and material she could ill afford at this time. The stirring of nationalist hopes among the Arabs in her North African territories has made the development of these areas an urgent problem, requiring among other steps an accelerated program of public capital investment. Carrying out these various projects during a period of worldwide raw material shortage and continuous pressure for higher standards of living for labor and low-income groups has been an exceedingly difficult task for a country whose capital resources were so severely depleted at the conclusion of hostilities.

While the financial problems of France have been heavy—perhaps disproportionately so—they have been offset to a considerable extent by the very substantial amount of assistance she has received. From the United States alone France secured nearly $5 billion in grants and loans from 1945 to the end of 1952, plus additional amounts for "offshore procurement" and the purchase or supply of goods and services for military and civilian use abroad. Borrowing from the International Bank for Reconstruction and Development and the International Monetary Fund and maximum use of the short-term credit available through the European Payments Union are among the other sources of assistance which France has utilized. Despite this aid, France is apparently not much nearer to a solution of her internal fiscal problems or her external payments difficulties than at the outset of the postwar period, and one must look further than the past decade for a full explanation of her continuing debility.

Psychological Factors

The root causes for the present situation go deep, and extend far beyond purely economic factors into the realm of the psychological. With nations, as with individuals, the course of development can be set as decisively by emotional forces as by logical economic considerations, though in most instances there is a blend of influence which defies precise labeling. The result is an amalgam of economic and psychological factors, which interact to color political decisions. In France, unfortunately, these factors have tended to reinforce rather than counteract each other. Economic problems, serious in themselves, have become even more critical because the French, as a nation, have been beset by fear: fear of a dynamic, expanding Germany, most obviously, but distrust of each other as well.

Out of this fear have grown the cynicism and concern with short-run advantages which have all but destroyed the sense of civic responsibility. "Cheating the government," which was fair game during the Occupation, is still a common practice, resulting in widespread tax evasion which accentuates the inequities of the revenue system and contributes to the further maldistribution of wealth and income.

Safeguards against the abuse of political power, incorporated into the Fourth Republic's constitution, have given the country an electoral law and a form of government in which fragmentized political groups hold the balance of power and imperil the life of any government encroaching upon their interests. As a result, there have been eighteen changes of Premier and cabinet during the past nine years, a constant reshuffling of authority which has obstructed the normal day-to-day activities of government and made basic reforms impossible.

In adjusting to the insecurity of the present, the French are following a familiar regression pattern, looking backward to their days of glory and clinging to the symbols of an outmoded way of living. Because there is no political or economic stability and no confidence in the future, there is little incentive to invest in new enterprises, and savings are put into gold hoards that can be locked up in strong boxes or hidden behind the chimneys. The people are slow to improve their techniques of production and distribution, not only because of the cost of modern equipment but also because of their fear of innovation. Economic policies tend toward an excessive reliance upon central authority, and a preference for a small, protected market in which competition is reduced to a minimum. Labor, as well as management, is reluctant to learn new ways of improving its efficiency, and is satisfied to have its inadequate wages supplemented by an elaborate system of social payments at fixed rates.

It would be strange indeed if there were no exceptions to these blanket generalizations; in fact, there have been numerous examples of individual courage and imagination which indicate what effective leadership might accomplish. Paradoxically, it was from the pervasive atmosphere of fear and despair in France that the idea of the Schuman Plan emerged, to become Western Europe's first brilliant venture in international economic integration. It is still too early to tell whether the ideals set forth in the charter of the European Coal and Steel Community will be achieved, but as the hard facts of competitive life become more apparent to French producers, enthusiasm for the project appears to be waning.

There is now little likelihood that France will support any move toward the political unification of the Community which was intended to be the second step forward. For a brief time during 1952, it seemed that M. Pinay might rally the electorate behind his efforts to set France upon a sound economic and fiscal course, but in this instance also the era of optimism and confidence under his leadership was of short duration.

Economic Factors

But what of the economic causes of this disturbing psychological climate? Is it possible to strengthen France's economic structure to such an extent as to lessen her insecurity and moderate her fears? Can she again become a forward-looking, dynamic nation? Undoubtedly France has the human and physical resources necessary for a prosperous, well-balanced economy, but there is urgent need for far-reaching reforms in her basic structure and institutions if these objectives are to be achieved.

As the French themselves freely admit, their economy has no flexibility. Though the world has changed markedly in the past thirty years, as new ideas and new productive techniques have brought major shifts in economic activity, France is still following essentially the same pattern as in the earlier period. She has the unique distinction of being the only important world power with a static population and a labor force that was actually five per cent smaller in 1952 than in 1921.

So far as occupations are concerned, there has been relatively little change. There has been a slight decline, it is true, in the numbers engaged in agriculture, but this still remains the most important single occupation, employing slightly more than a third of the total working population. Significantly, perhaps, the shift from the farms has been entirely to the trade and service industries, rather than to manufacturing. The number of industrial workers has remained virtually unchanged from the 1920's to the present, and the only source of increase in factory labor has been the employment of those formerly out of work.

Despite the recent efforts to modernize production and distribution techniques and encourage large-scale operations, small businesses still predominate in all sectors of the French economy. Largely as a result of French inheritance laws, there has been a tendency for agricultural lands to be split up into small widely-scattered plots. About 80 per cent of the farms are under fifty acres, which is regarded as the minimum on which a tractor can be economically used full-time, and more than half are twenty-five acres or less.

In industry and commerce, also, the small enterprise is the most common. France is not only "a nation of small shopkeepers"—about three-fourths of her commercial establishments are individual proprietorships without other wage-earning employees—but also a nation of small factories, with less than 1,100 industrial plants employing 500 or more workers in 1950. As a result of small-scale activities, production and distribution costs are high, and manufactured goods are likely to be luxury items which involve considerable handwork and offer little possibility for standardization. The production system is keyed to a high unit profit on small output for a limited local market.

It was apparent as early as the 1930's that France was not keeping pace with her neighbors. Most of the industrialized countries of the world had recovered from depression and reached new high levels of activity during the late 1930's, but France, pursuing her high-cost, small-scale method of operations, was still producing 10-20 per cent less than in 1929 as late as 1938. It was not until 1951 and 1952, when her few modern postwar plants came into production, that France finally surpassed the 1929 record.

In the fiscal area, also, there has been little effort to change outmoded concepts and practices. France still has an ineffective, regressive system of taxation, and still displays a persistent tendency to meet chronic budget deficits through inflationary methods. Direct taxation accounts for only a fourth of the government's revenue, and consists largely of income taxes upon corporate business and industrial wage earners, without a proportionate contribution from the farmers, small tradesmen and professional workers whose income cannot be successfully tapped at the source. The government relies chiefly, therefore, upon indirect taxes, including customs duties, production and transaction taxes, taxes on matches and other government monopolies, which currently contribute nearly 60 per cent of its total income. These taxes are, of course, passed on to the ultimate consumers and add appreciably to the final selling price of merchandise.

That price, in addition, must also cover the heavy burden of social security charges, which, it is estimated, amount to about 45 per cent of labor costs. Despite these levies upon employers, the social security system is not self-supporting, and its annual deficits are a factor in France's continuous budgetary problems. Since 1913, there have been only four years, 1926 to 1929, when government income has equalled government expenditure. Though the size of the budget deficits in the postwar period has been unusual because of the abnormally high expenditures on reconstruction and the Indo-Chinese War, the fact of budget imbalance is nothing new in France. Nor is the continuous rise in the national debt which has resulted from Treasury borrowing, at home and abroad, to meet these recurrent deficits. Much of this borrowing has led directly to an expansion of the monetary and credit supply, adding further stimulus to the inflationary pressures with which France has had to contend.

Inflation

Although the problem of inflation has been especially severe in recent years, the phenomenon of rising prices has been a familiar one in France during the greater part of the last half century. At the present time, the index of wholesale prices has reached a level of 178 times that of July, 1914, compared with a four-fold increase in the United States over the same period. The first upsurge in prices came during and after World War I, reaching its climax in 1926 when the index averaged slightly more than 700 (July, 1914=100). About half of this rise was erased in the subsequent depression period, but from 1935 to date prices have continued to move upward, the sharpest rises occurring from the conclusion of World War II to 1951.

This was a period when demand for goods was far in excess of supplies, not only in France but elsewhere throughout the world. The restoration of war-shattered areas, the satisfaction of pent-up demands for both capital and consumer goods, the pressure for higher standards of living for the underprivileged in industrialized as well as in undeveloped countries, all occurring at a time when production of peace-time goods was low and the supply of money large, meant inevitable shortages and rising prices which burst the bonds of rationing and price controls.

In France the situation was especially acute, not only because of the great extent of war damage she had suffered, but also because of the added strain which her domestic modernization program and her heavy defense expenditures at home and in Indo-China placed upon her depleted resources. Possibly a more determined effort to cope with the inflationary problem might have moderated the rise in prices, but the record shows that the sporadic, half-hearted attempts to deal with the situation were invariably too little and too late.

Labor, in a strong bargaining position due to the loss of some 12 per cent of the working force as prisoners of war, casualties or deportees, has apparently succeeded in keeping wage rates geared to the advance in the official cost-of-living index, which has been kept low by virtue of government subsidies on many foodstuffs and price controls upon others. It is doubtful, however, that the worker's purchasing power in real terms has been maintained. Certainly, the inequities of inflation have widened the cleavage between industry and agriculture; between labor and employer; and between labor and agriculture, on the one hand, and the group of white-collar workers, government employees and small investors, on the other.

The private capital market has disappeared, since savings now go into sterile hoards rather than investment. Except where the government has financed postwar modernization and expansion, or industry has ploughed back its profits, capital equipment is worn out and obsolete. There is little opportunity for increased labor productivity, therefore, and most of the higher wages won by labor have been passed along to the consumer in the form of higher prices. Partly as a result of declining world raw material prices, partly as a result of M. Pinay's and M. Laniel's efforts to reduce internal inflationary forces, the French price level has shown signs of stability recently, but no far-reaching reforms have been undertaken, and none seem likely under present political conditions.

Foreign Trade

The problem of inflation and its attendant evils would be sufficiently serious if it were confined solely to internal relationships; it becomes critically important, however, through its effect upon foreign trade and payments. Traditionally, France has been less dependent than most of the countries in Western Europe upon foreign trade. With a high ratio of land to population, and a wide range of natural resources, France and her North African territories have supplied about 85 per cent of her food requirements and many of her industrial raw materials as well. Though she has needed to import such essential commodities as coke, oil, rubber, textile fibers, metals (except iron and aluminum) and wood pulp and paper, her exports of luxury-type goods, plus her income from such "invisibles" as shipping, tourism and foreign investments, have enabled her to secure these products in the limited volume required by her domestic industries.

Her industrial development, as we have seen, progressed slowly, despite periodic attempts to widen and improve industrial capacity, and production was primarily for the home market. In 1938, for example, exports of iron and steel products, including machinery and vehicles, accounted for only 17 per cent of the total value of French exports, compared with 36 per cent for the United States and 29 per cent for the United Kingdom. Lack of a well-developed heavy industry meant, also, that France had to import most of the capital equipment needed by her manufacturers.

This pattern of trade proved satisfactory only during periods of comparative prosperity abroad, and signs of strain have been apparent whenever the demand for French luxuries contracted, or tourists remained at home. The situation has been most critical, of course, during the years immediately following World War I and, again, in the post-World War II period, when French import requirements have been at a maximum and export capabilities at a minimum. But even during the 1930's, when most of Europe had recovered its pre-depression levels of industrial activity, French export markets revived at a lagging pace and the resulting payments difficulties contributed to France's inability to regain her 1929 volume of production. To meet recurrent payments deficits France exported gold, borrowed extensively abroad, imposed quotas upon her imports, developed her protected export markets in the overseas territories, and, as a final measure, resorted frequently to currency devaluation. Through these measures she achieved an uneasy equilibrium in her payments position, but failed to strike at the basic cause of the problem: inefficient, high-cost production of relatively non-essential goods.

Postwar Payments Problems

The payments problems which France has faced since the end of World War II have dwarfed those of earlier years in magnitude and complexity. Because of the complete disruption of her economy, she has needed substantial imports of food as well as of consumer goods and capital equipment. Colonial territories, whose requirements would normally be met by French manufacturers, had to be supplied from hard-currency areas, but could produce little for an offsetting export to these markets. Tourist income was negligible and the loss of her merchant fleet, a prewar source of profit, necessitated large expenditure on freight and transportation. France dipped heavily into her remaining gold and foreign exchange reserves to finance her abnormally high import requirements for the years 1945, 1946 and 1947, but though her resources were depleted to the danger point at that time, reconstruction was still far from complete.

Two events occurring in 1947 set the course for subsequent developments in France. One—the adoption by the United States of the Marshall Plan for dollar assistance to our Western European allies—provided a temporary solution for France's continuing payments problem; the other—the adoption by France of the Monnet Plan for the modernization and expansion of a half-dozen or so of her basic industries—was an attempt to create a modern industrial economy upon the ashes of prewar lethargy and postwar confusion. To a considerable extent these programs have been interrelated, for Marshall Plan dollars have enabled France to finance the imports of capital goods necessary to put the Monnet Plan into effect.

For the ensuing five years, the stimulus of American aid and large-scale investment expenditure appeared to have set France upon her economic feet. Industrial production expanded as the targets for coal, oil, electricity, steel and cement were approached, and by 1952, the output of industrial goods was 45 per cent larger than in 1938 and 16 per cent above the 1929 peak. Dollar assistance, in reduced amount and restricted largely to military procurement, appeared adequate to meet a narrowing dollar gap.

Although the first Monnet Plan represents the most constructive effort to date to revitalize the French economy, the optimism engendered by its apparent successes up to mid-1952 has been dispelled by later developments. The increasing severity of payments problems in non-dollar areas, primarily in sterling and other Western European currencies, and the sharp decline in consumer goods production, which took place in the latter half of 1952 and continued during 1953, point up how far France still remains from viability, and how far she must still go to correct her structural weaknesses. Except in her newest plants, costs are still too high, and French exports tend to seek non-competitive markets within the French Union. Little has been done to improve the productivity of agriculture, and food costs absorb a disproportionate share of consumers' income, thus limiting the purchasing power available for other products. Consumer goods industries, also, need to become more efficient and to rely less upon tariffs, import quotas and other restrictive devices to protect their local markets. The idle capital resources of the country must be lured from hiding by evidence of sound fiscal policies and monetary stability so that privately financed investment may be substituted for government expenditure. These are problems to which the Second Monnet Plan must direct its attention.

Enthusiasm and Confidence Required

Above all, France needs a psychological rebirth. As the Europeans who have toured American industrial centers in search of the secrets of our productivity have discovered, the most important element in dynamic economic progress is found in the attitude of the workers at all levels of the production process. Better equipment, more efficient techniques, accomplish little unless they are employed with "the sense of adventurous urgency," which one observer felt to be the distinguishing characteristic of the American scene. In France, to an even greater extent than in other industrialized countries, both management and labor must strive to create a counterpart to what another European described as the "atmosphere of self-reliant ambition" that prevails in the United States. Only if the fear of innovation and of technological unemployment can be replaced by enthusiasm and confidence can the chains which bind France to the past be broken.

The most encouraging factor in the present situation is that the French, themselves, recognize the need for a change in the psychological climate. In its review of the achievements of the First Monnet Plan and its suggestions for the future, the Commissariat General which has administered the program includes this significant observation: "The attitude of ordinary individuals, of the professions, the banks and the public authorities is to give priority to security and to the maintenance of what status they have achieved—a state of mind which has contributed to a kind of sclerosis of the whole nation that can only prevent any response . . . to the need for new industrial techniques and the pressure for higher living standards . . . Investments will have an essential part to play; but they must be accompanied by reforms that will eliminate all that is paralyzing and sterilizing the economic apparatus . . . The first plan brought the country face to face with the alternative: modernize or decay. The second plan will have fulfilled its purpose if it leads the French nation to grasp the opportunity for a better future and to put this goal ahead of clinging for protection to the mediocre *status quo.*"

Potentialities for Greatness

At the moment, the outlook is weighted with pessimism. France may indeed be "in 1788," as M. Mendes-France declared, facing the necessity for reforms in institutions, in methods and in attitudes which are, perhaps, as far-reaching as those of the Revolution. But one need look no further than to the record of accomplishment during the 1946-1951 period to realize the potentialities for greatness which France still possesses. The problems of the present, though critical, are primarily problems of organization, where each constructive step can be expected to bring substantial progress.

For an effective attack upon these structural weaknesses, France must have inspired leadership—not necessarily Mr. Baldwin's "second Napoleon," but leadership of sufficient strength to bridge the deep cleavages in the social and political structure and channel the creative talents of the country into the new patterns required of a modern industrialized state. If courage and self-confidence can be revived, if the dynamism of the early postwar years can be recaptured, France may again become a pillar of strength in the free world coalition.

M. Janice Murphy

POSTWAR INTRA-EUROPEAN PAYMENTS INSTITUTIONS

As the early postwar dollar shortage persisted, it became imperative that intra-European trade be revived or even expanded. The countries of Western Europe had to secure a larger percentage of their essential imports from each other and fewer from the dollar areas.

In their foreign exchange relationships with one another since 1947, these nations have progressed from rigid bilateralism to relatively flexible regionalism. To most Americans, the slow and somewhat irregular steps by which this limited progress has been accomplished have been overshadowed by other more publicized political and economic developments. Successive endeavors to alleviate or overcome intra-regional payments barriers, however, have played an interesting and significant part in promoting trade and production among the Western European countries.

Not as well known as the dollar shortage, but just as important for the trade of the countries involved, was the inconvertibility of the Western European currencies even among themselves. For some countries there was a Belgian franc or British pound shortage, while for others it was a Swedish kronor or French franc shortage. Under such circumstances, it was almost as difficult to finance foreign exchange requirements within Western Europe as it was with the dollar area. In most countries the gold and dollar reserves were so low that some technique had to be developed to reduce or eliminate recourse to such reserves in intra-European payments.

The first attempt to solve the problem of securing materials essential for recovery programs, in spite of the foreign exchange difficulties, was a network of bilateral trade and payments agreements. Imports and exports outlined in the agreements were expected to offset each other to such an extent that the necessity for any gold payments would be substantially reduced. Further to conserve gold and dollar holdings, limited credit margins (or swing accounts) were established to finance seasonal trade fluctuations which caused temporary payments deficits for one of the partner countries.

Although the bilateral framework permitted restoration of some trade in Western Europe, its overall effectiveness was extremely limited. By the summer of 1947, most of the credit margins were exhausted. Cyclical fluctuations often failed to materialize in the balances of payments between pairs of countries. Too frequently export surpluses tended to run in one direction, such as a persistent Belgian surplus with Great Britain, rather than to reverse themselves periodically. Moreover, bilateralism meant that trade surpluses earned with one country could not, as a rule, be used to cover trade deficits with others. The trade debtors then faced the alternatives of settling their future deficits in gold or of reducing imports from their creditors. Inadequate gold and dollar reserves usually forced such debtors to choose the latter policy. Continuation of this tendency could, of course, only mean a downward spiral in the level of intra-regional trade—a trend that both the creditors and debtors in Western Europe had sought to avoid when they originally resorted to bilateralism.

Sterling Convertibility

European financial morale was temporarily raised in the summer of 1947 when the British authorities announced current account convertibility of sterling.[1] Any country exporting goods to the United Kingdom or to any other member of the sterling area could request payment either in sterling or in dollars. Western European creditor countries thought that they then would be able to convert their net intra-European trade surpluses into sterling and then into dollars, thus reducing their own dollar shortages. That possibility was based on the assumptions that the United Kingdom would maintain its import surplus from Western Europe and that sterling would remain convertible. Unfortunately,

[1]Convertibility was one of the British obligations under the 1946 American Loan to the United Kingdom of $3.75 billions.

only five weeks later sterling convertibility was cancelled because of its heavy drain on the British gold and dollar reserves.

This premature and unsuccessful "dash for freedom" by means of sterling convertibility served both to undermine confidence in sterling and to reveal weaknesses in the other European currencies. Its psychological impact is still evident today in the caution with which British and Continental financial authorities view any definite proposals for a precipitous return to even current account convertibility of sterling. Those officials tend to advocate convertibility only if it is accompanied by strict controls over the direction of trade and by a large stabilization or reserve fund of dollars.

Inauguration of ERP

Another approach to Western Europe's problem of securing essential imports evolved with the inauguration of the multibillion dollar European Recovery Program in 1948. With the assurance of resources, mostly in the form of free imports from the dollar area, the countries could proceed with their basic recovery and expansion programs. One of the most significant features introduced by the Marshall Plan was the establishment of the Organization for European Economic Cooperation (OEEC). It was given the responsibility for dividing the Marshall Plan credits among the sixteen member countries after attempting to evaluate and to coordinate the various national programs. This responsibility and the availability of extensive dollar-area resources promoted continuous cooperation among the Western European governments on regional economic policies.

As a result of the cooperative approach to common problems, limited multilateralism was introduced into the financial settlements of intra-European trade in the fall of 1948. Both the 1948 and the 1949 Payments and Compensations Agreements required the signatory countries to report their individual bilateral surpluses and deficits with every other OEEC member to the Bank for International Settlements at the end of each month. The Bank then computed the amounts which could be cleared from the sum of intra-European payments indebtedness without giving rise to any new bilateral surplus or deficit positions. Although this technique allowed a country to use some of its earnings from bilateral surpluses to cover part of its bilateral deficits, the magnitude of the offsetting was quantitatively small in terms of the payments disequilibria within Western Europe. Residual amounts of bilateral indebtedness were then settled either by "drawing rights" or by some combination of credits and gold payments according to the terms of the bilateral agreements between each pair of countries.

Certain countries in Western Europe agreed to extend credit in their own currencies (drawing rights) to specified weaker countries. The creditors were not altruistic in this contribution—they were required by the conditional aid clauses of the European Recovery Program authorizations to extend such drawing rights before receiving their full share of Marshall Plan dollars. Regardless of the motivating cause of these intra-European credits, they temporarily alleviated the most pressing problems associated with the inconvertibility of the Western European currencies with one another.

As the basis for further progress towards surmounting payments difficulties within Western Europe, however, the concept of offsetting debits and credits was more important than the drawing rights feature. No less important was the increasing tendency of the national officials to consult with one another about their own and others' economic problems, whether directly or only indirectly connected with regional trade. Although both the 1948 and the 1949 Agreements introduced substantial improvements over the exclusively bilateral arrangements that preceded them, balance of payments settlements within Western Europe still remained largely on a bilateral basis. Drawing rights were established in only one direction between each pair of countries. They were not, therefore, available for settlement purposes if the predicted patterns of trade did not develop. Also, the credit-gold provisions for handling residual balances were, as mentioned previously, governed by the bilateral agreements.

European Payments Union

Just as the Marshall Plan neared the half-way point in terms of time and recovery accomplishments, the recipient nations undertook negotiations for a new method to facilitate intra-European payments. Because the countries varied so much from one another in their basic economic philosophies, their respective proposals were frequently contradictory. The Belgian-led "hard-money" school, which emphasized orthodox fiscal and monetary policies, conflicted with the "soft-currency" countries led by the United Kingdom, which stressed the importance of full employment and welfare criteria even at the expense of balance of payments difficulties and inflationary monetary policies. Nevertheless, after six months of continuous negotiations, the OEEC countries drafted and agreed to a series of compromises, which were facilitated by their previous cooperation in the OEEC and by American financial assistance. In September, 1950, the purposes and mechanisms of a new regional financial institution were formalized in the Agreement for the Establishment of a European Payments Union (EPU).

In direct contrast to the preceding schemes, which were annually negotiated and thus obviously temporary, the new Union was expected to function even after the scheduled end of the Marshall Plan in 1952. For the first time, a free-world area directly challenged the 1944 Bretton Woods decision to establish only one intergovernmental institution (the International Monetary Fund), to assist countries with balance of payments problems, individually rather than by regions. Unlike the International Monetary Fund which was based on a universal membership (i.e., open to all countries which agreed to certain minimum conditions), the European Payments Union is restricted to Western European countries. However, its financial operations are applicable to the entire monetary areas of the participating nations—e.g., the sterling area and the French franc area. Its purpose is to provide a central clearing institution for the complete financial settlement of all trade surpluses and deficits between the respective currency areas, and a periodic (usually monthly) examination of the payments position of all its members.

Settlements are based upon a member's net cumulative position with the area as a whole. Therefore, it is no longer necessary for members to watch their trading relationships with each of the other fifteen members of the OEEC. Instead, they can concentrate on their balance with Western Europe as a whole, which means that they can purchase imports on the basis of comparative prices alone rather than on a combination of prices and foreign exchange availabilities, at least within the region.

Each member of the EPU has a quota which limits the extent of its gold and credit obligations and rights. As a country moves through its quota, it receives or pays an increasing percentage of gold, depending upon whether it is a cumulative creditor or a cumulative debtor. The graduated credit-gold ratios automatically exert financial pressure on the countries with extreme payments positions within the region. Although historical and theoretical evidence indicates that some degree of imbalance is usually beneficial, in economic terms, to all members of a region, it was not feasible from 1950 to 1953 to permit the imbalance to develop haphazardly. The gold and dollar reserves of the EPU as well as those of the member countries were insufficient to cover large disequilibria. Moreover, in so far as Europe intends to pursue regionalism rather than universalism in its long-range trade policies, measures that would promote intra-regional balance for each member would be most desirable.

Full Convertibility the Goal

However, the EPU Agreement explicitly states that the objective of the signatory countries is gradually to increase the liberalization and multilateralization of trade and payments within Western Europe until full convertibility is restored, not only among the respective European currencies but even with the dollar currencies. The technique is to increase the competitive potential of Western European industries by gradually exposing their respective economies to the products and thus to the efficiencies of other member countries. In the process, the most efficient industries should be able to expand their basic markets and thus obtain the economies of scale, such as mass production techniques. By increasing the capacity and productivity of their most efficient industries, the OEEC countries should be able to compete more effectively with dollar area goods in Western Europe as well as in third markets. Since multilateralism, not regionalism, is the ultimate trading objective of the EPU members, certain countries, such as Belgium, were allowed to continue surplus positions while others, like France, have accumulated deficits in their payments positions with Western Europe.

To finance any discrepancy between the amount of gold which debtors might pay to the Union and the amount of gold which the Union has to pay to the creditors, the EPU is empowered to draw upon the $350 million reserve fund which the United States Government placed at its disposal. However, the reserve fund plus other special dollar resources are insufficient to finance persistent extreme positions.[2] Therefore, the Managing Board of the EPU, composed of independent experts, continually analyzes the domestic and regional pressures which might contribute to

---

[2]Other special resources granted to Austria, France, Greece, Iceland and Turkey by the American Government to cover part of their EPU deficits amounted to $354 million by the end of December, 1953.

severe payments disequilibria. Upon the basis of these analyses, the Managing Board makes oral or written recommendations to the member countries directly or to the OEEC Council, when modifications of the normal operation of the Union require the latter's approval.

Influence Upon Domestic Policies

Political and financial officials of the member countries were usually willing and able to implement the recommendations of the Managing Board even when they referred to traditionally domestic factors such as fiscal and commercial policies. National acceptance of regional influence was highlighted by the case of Western Germany as a debtor with the region. In the spring months of 1951, a board of independent non-German experts was established by the EPU to supervise the day-to-day allocations of German foreign exchange earnings. Although this particular technique was not repeated with other debtors, substantial co-operation and frequent consultation developed between the regional and national authorities on matters such as increasing imports from countries which temporarily lost intra-European markets, decreasing imports from nations which already had extreme creditor positions, and encouraging national anti-inflationary credit policies.

Two factors help to explain such influence upon domestic policies. Because the members of the Managing Board are generally recognized as outstanding experts, their publicized recommendations command a position of respect in Western Europe. Much more important, however, is the OEEC Trade Liberalization Code. It provides that any relaxation of import quotas must be applied in a non-discriminatory fashion to all EPU exporters. Thus, if a country withdraws from the EPU, it might encounter discriminatory restrictions against its usual exports to the region. This, undoubtedly, was a major factor in the continued participation of nations like Belgium in an organization which requires the creditor countries to extend large amounts of credit to the Union. An extreme debtor likewise remains in the Union even when it exceeds its quota and thus has to make 100 per cent gold payments for all further deficits. Such a debtor is allowed to reimpose import restrictions when its gold and dollar reserves are seriously threatened, without the likelihood that other members will retaliate by raising restrictions against its exports.

It is almost impossible to assess the exact contribution of regional endeavors, like the EPU, to increased trade between members of the region. Part of that increase may have been caused by recovery and expansion of domestic production and purchasing power levels, part by the unpredictable vicissitudes of trading patterns, and part by the basic trends of recent commercial history. Nevertheless, there can be little doubt but that financial facilities of the EPU largely eliminated the foreign-exchange justifications for restrictions on intra-European trade that existed in the earlier postwar years. Similarly, the financial resources of the Union facilitated the operation of the OEEC trade liberalization program which was designed to increase competitive pressures within the region. Western Europe's improved ability to compete with American products can now be seen in the expanding gold and dollar reserves of the individual countries and, especially, in the increasing number of American producers' complaints against imports from Europe into the United States.

Questions for the Future

More and more attention has been directed recently towards the desirability and requirements of another convertibility attempt for sterling, and perhaps for the Belgian franc and the German mark, at least on current account transactions. This possibility not only raises the problem of how convertibility might affect the operations and even the existence of the EPU, but also a host of other questions. If certain countries have sufficient overall equilibrium in their balances of payments and have adequate reserves to cover any predictable fluctuations in their payments positions, should they be encouraged to travel the road to convertibility gradually or immediately, alone or in unison with all or some of the other EPU members? Even if some countries are, or become, ready for immediate convertibility for current trade transactions, what will happen to those countries which not only remain debtors within Western Europe but also have heavy deficits with outside areas?

Western Europe must now choose among several alternatives: (1) further reduction of trade barriers within the EPU area; (2) reduction of restrictions on imports from the dollar area while maintaining the present level of barriers in Europe; or (3) full convertibility rights for all proceeds from all current transactions with all areas. In essence, the governments concerned must decide if the time is ripe for abandonment of regionalism and adoption of universal multilateralism.

Marjorie S. Belcher

TOWN FINANCE IN SEVENTEENTH CENTURY PLYMOUTH

Plymouth, Massachusetts, today is a town of about ten thousand inhabitants, with an annual budget of approximately two and a half million dollars. Three hundred years ago Plymouth was a village of less than five hundred inhabitants, one of about a dozen such villages in the Plymouth Colony. Functions and budgets of all levels of government have increased manyfold since the seventeenth century. Thus it is rather surprising that, although it is impossible to estimate from town records[1] the total annual town expenditures in the 1600's, there were taxes levied and expenditures authorized then for purposes which fit into the broad categories which today account for about 70 per cent of the town's budget. Public service enterprises, recreation, health and sanitation, cemeteries and veterans' benefits are the only important town functions today for which there was nothing comparable three hundred years ago.

Education and Protection

Public schools today account for more than one-quarter of the town's expenditures. Schools first entered the town's budget when the town of Plymouth took advantage of the offer of the Colony in 1670 to make available the proceeds of the lease of Cape Cod Bay fishing for free schools in the towns within the

[1]The records of the Town of Plymouth were published by order of the town in 1889. Volume I covers from 1636 to 1705 and consists primarily of records of land deeds and of the actions taken at town meetings. Most of the information included here is taken from this volume.

colony. In 1672 it was voted in town meeting that the profits and benefits from two pieces of town land should be used toward the maintenance of the "free scoole now begun and erected att Plymouth." This marked what is believed to have been the beginning of the first completely free public school in New England. The school remained free only until 1677 when some charges were imposed, although the town continued to contribute to school maintenance. Free schooling was not provided again in Plymouth until 1704.

The ten percent of the town budget today which is devoted to protection of persons and property covers the expenses of the tree warden and the police and fire departments. None of these was a town function in the seventeenth century. Protection of persons and property then required that each man serve his turn at the watch maintained at the fort, and pay a special tax for the building and equipping of the fort. In addition to the tax, each man was required to supply "two peeces more of viii foote long to finish the fortyfycacon."

Protection of persons and property in the 1680's also included the costs of the legal defense of Plymouth's right to Clark's Island in the harbor when Sir Edmond Andros visited New England to claim for the king the title to all public lands not specifically granted in the charter. Plymouth's charter and patent rights were confused during most of the period until the Plymouth Colony was merged with the Massachusetts Bay Colony in 1691, and resistance to Andros' claim involved costs which were met by a series of tax levies and eventually by sale of the island into private ownership.

Welfare Expenditures

Care of the poor was a major town expenditure in the seventeenth century as in the twentieth. Today about twenty-five per cent of town expenditures are classified as charities, including public welfare and care of the aged. However, town charity was somewhat more personal in colonial times. For example, in 1636 the town meeting voted a voluntary collection for Richard Willis who "by his long sickness is growne very weake and in great want."

When, in 1649, it was agreed that all town business could not be conducted by general town meetings, a group of seven men were chosen to govern the town. These select men were given responsibility for inquiring into the state of the poor, using their best discretion in caring for them and, if necessary, levying taxes for their relief.

Care of the poor itemized in town expenditures for any year consisted usually of payments to individual townsmen for the care of a needy individual. For example, town charges for 1695/6 include "For Joseph Bartlet for Keeping Nan Ramsden. . . 6 pounds" and two other items of one pound and a few shillings each to others for care of Nan Ramsden. The next year John Nelson was paid five pounds for keeping her for a year, after which she drops out of town records.

On rare occasions, the town went further than paying each year for the support of a public charge. In 1679 Samuel Jenny was granted the watch house "in respect of his destitute condition to be for a house for him to dwell in and not to be sold or estranged to any other use." Since a new fort had been erected a few years before, this may have been a practical way of using a building which had served its original purpose.

Costs of General Government

The costs of general government in the seventeenth century included contributions to the support of the Colony—even as today Plymouth's town budget includes payment of State and county assessments. From Cape Cod the Colony of New Plymouth extended north to a much disputed boundary with the Massachusetts Bay Colony near Cohasset and west to the Providence Plantations. Until the Bay Colony's new charter in 1691 merged the two colonies, Plymouth Colony was a separate governmental unit. Colonial revenues from the lease of fishing rights and proceeds from trading and hunting outposts in Maine did not cover the costs of official colonial business, and the Colony regularly asked funds from the various towns within its borders.

Other general town expenses included salaries of a growing list of town officials—the select men, the constable, the surveyors, the town clerk, town treasurer, the fence viewers—payments to those who served on juries, and such incidentals as janitorial service for the meeting house and ringing of the town bell. In 1953 such general government costs amounted to five per cent of total expenditures, or slightly more than $100,000.

Support of Religion

One important town expenditure in the seventeenth century which is no longer a matter of town finance was the support of the minister and th emeeting house. It is difficult to judge whether contributions to such costs were voluntary or mandatory. The records contain numerous entries of raters appointed to determine each individual's share of the minister's salary voted at the town meeting. Nevertheless, early histories indicate that these contributions were in fact voluntary and that the order by the General Court of the Colony in 1678 that a house of worship be erected in each town and village was the first compulsory collection of taxes for the support of the ministry.

In some towns in the Colony the minister was given responsibility for collecting the tax levied for his salary, thus apparently making the tax a voluntary contribution unless the minister was a forceful tax collector. One indication of the semi-voluntary nature of such taxes is the action of the town meeting on January 26, 1663, regarding collection of funds already voted for building a house for the minister. The meeting voted that the few who "may scruple the way of gathering or levying the said sume by rate" might make whatever contribution they wished, which could be accepted if it seemed reasonable to those responsible for collection of the funds.

Whether contributions to support of religion were required by law or only required by social pressure, adequate provision for the minister required frequent action by town meetings. In addition to voting a salary every year and providing fire wood, the town on occasion voted to pay the costs of moving a minister and his family from their last parish. When at last in 1667 Plymouth found a minister who stayed for a number of years, the minister was as concerned for the future security of his family as the town was with keeping the minister contented. Several years later the minister's house, built at town expense, was voted given to the minister and his heirs. The town's generosity was rewarded, for the minister remained for thirty years, far longer than any other during the early years of the colony.

Revenues

Plymouth today depends on the real estate and personal property tax for more than half of its revenues. The bulk of the other half comes from payments for water, cemeteries, and public service enterprises. The poll tax brings in less than $10,000 and in 1953, when the town was not engaged in any major construction, the proceeds of bond issues were less than $150,000.

In the seventeenth century, sale of town land and income from a long list of fines provided some revenue; the town also had the equivalent of revenue in the required labor of able-bodied men on such projects as repair of the fort and highway maintenance. However, taxation was by far the major source of revenue.

Occasionally the basis for levying the tax was directly related to the purpose of the tax. For example, the payment of half a penny to the killer of each wolf was required of each person except "the poore that have not cattell." The first tax for maintenance of the roads in the early 1700's was clearly a substitute for required labor and was levied equally on all able-bodied men.

In the early years of the town, the basis for levying general taxes was left to the raters appointed to collect them. This soon proved unsatisfactory and in 1667 the town meeting directed the select men to study the basis for levying taxes and to report to the town at a subsequent meeting. Three years later, probably on the basis of this report, the town adopted a detailed plan of assessment which established basic rules for valuation of real estate and cattle and made a start at establishing the basis for taxation of those whose income did not come from land.

Every man was required to submit a bill of estate to the raters as a basis for assessment. Rules were agreed upon to value land on the basis of its distance from the center of town and the extent of clearing and cultivation. Cattle values were set, depending upon age and sex, and the value of weavers' looms, fishermen's boats and tailors' "faculties" were determined on the basis of the extent of their use. Thus John Fallowey's loom was valued at less than that of other weavers because it was "not so constantly Imployed." All single men with estates valued at less than eighteen pounds were, nevertheless, to be taxed on the basis of eighteen pounds. Two years later, the faculties of the various coopers, carpenters, innkeepers and smiths were given a set value for tax purposes. A rough measure of ability to pay had been established as the basis for levying the general taxes of the town.

Collection of Taxes

The duties of levying and collecting taxes fell upon raters appointed for each individual tax. Thus at any given time there were often several groups of raters combining the functions of assessors, tax collectors, and even constables, but only in connection with a single tax levy.

Taxes were usually collected in goods rather than currency.

For example, the first tax described in the Town Record, voted in 1640, was the relevying on the men of the town of Plymouth's share of the tax in corn levied by the Colony on the towns of Plymouth and Green Harbor. Such "countrey pay" created complications in the collection of the tax. For example, town action in 1641 regarding the bounty paid for killing of wolves within the town provided that the half penny levied on each person should be paid to the miller who should, on receipt of the wolf skin, pay the hunter in corn and keep the skin as payment for "his paynes in delivering forth the corne."

Firm price lists and schedules for payments had also to be established. One of the more complicated was that voted by the town in providing for the minister's salary in 1668. The salary of 80 pounds was required to be paid one-third in wheat or butter, one-third in rye, barley or peas, and one-third in Indian corn. One-half of the salary was to be paid by the first of January, and the other half before the end of September. Prices were set for each of the commodities involved. A committee of raters trying to insure that their collections for this tax came to the prescribed proportions of each product and were collected in time to meet the minister's needs could hardly have been asked to carry on the same operations simultaneously in connection with another tax.

Forward Planning—The Greatest Change

Probably the main reason for having separate raters for separate taxes, however, was simply that a tax was voted for one purpose without regard to any other taxes which might be needed during the same period. This lack of forward planning is the dominant impression gained from studying old town records. By 1700 Plymouth town government was a complex business involving a wide range of activities as reflected in the taxes and expenditures voted. Yet town expenditures and the taxes to meet them were voted only as the need arose. A town budget and a general tax assessment for a year were still in the future. One tax could be levied in corn because it was for a purpose for which payment in corn was acceptable. Only rarely were cash payments needed.

This simplicity and absence of need for anticipating the problems and expenses of the next twelve months would be much envied by the Advisory and Finance Committee of the town today, as they plan through one winter for the needs of the town for the year beginning the following spring.

Carol Colver

ECONOMIC BASES FOR POWER MARKETS IN THE PACIFIC NORTHWEST

Area economic surveys have been conducted by many agencies, for many purposes, and with varying degrees of comprehensiveness. The 30-odd county economic surveys conducted in the Pacific Northwest by the Bonneville Power Administration of the U. S. Department of Interior, however, were unique, I believe, in covering so large a proportion of a region with a truly comprehensive approach.

Originated for the purpose of estimating markets for hydroelectric power sold by the Administration, these surveys became cooperative regional projects, to which government agencies at Federal, state, county and city levels, businessmen, farmers and fishermen all contributed. They were more all-inclusive and analytical than "basic data sheets" which have been compiled for many sections of the country by government agencies or universities. They were not written to support foregone conclusions, as is sometimes the case with industrial location surveys prepared by private consultants.

Unfortunately, from the point of view of the economic historian, the work was discontinued in the middle of 1947, when an economy move by Congress abolished the Market Analysis Section before the work of surveying the region was completed. The value of such reports in administering a hydroelectric transmission system cannot, therefore, be appraised. How much use local people made of the reports in their own "grass roots" planning I do not know, although at the time many local groups urgently asked the Section to make these surveys for that purpose. But the methods used may still be of interest to the economic historian and to others engaged in projecting population trends. A very fragmentary test, based on the 1950 census, of the job and population estimates in four county surveys in which I participated, indicates that the methods used had considerable validity.

From 1943 to 1947 the Market Analysis Section of the Bonneville Power Administration published about 30 economic surveys for Washington, Oregon and Montana counties entitled "The Economic Base for Power Markets in XYZ County." The Administration was established to build, and sell power at wholesale from, a transmission system which connected into a single grid the lines from Grand Coulee and Bonneville Dams, facilities in which about $300 million was invested by the Federal Government. Since the war, the Administration has continued to tie into this grid lines from several other dams on the Columbia River system which at the time of the surveys were only on the drafting board.

Colonial Economy of the Northwest

The Pacific Northwest (Washington, Oregon, Idaho, and Montana), with only a century of white settlement behind it, has in some ways a colonial economy. It has the last large virgin timber stands in the United States. It has extensive fisheries. Its land is immensely productive. Vast areas around Grand Coulee Dam have still to yield their first crop when irrigation water flows from the reservoirs. Mineral resources are varied but, in Washington and Oregon, relatively untapped. Finally, there is the tremendous hydroelectric power potential of the Columbia River system. Its harnessing at Grand Coulee Dam came just in time to assist at the birth of atomic power, and made possible the manufacture of aluminum on a scale hitherto unimagined.

Thus, the economy is primarily dependent on natural resources, and a considerable proportion of its jobs are "extractive." Further, railway freight rates favor hauling many raw materials in bulk to the East for manufacture and handicap the sale of Western fabricated products in Eastern markets. Jobs and population in most of the counties surveyed were therefore estimated largely on the basis of potential production of natural resources. One of the biggest question marks was the commercial feasibility and probability of complete fabrication of these products in the Pacific Northwest region.

In each survey, the Market Analysis Section worked closely with regional offices of Federal agencies, state and county officials, chambers of commerce, and farm groups. Bringing together these diverse points of view stimulated a fairly objective viewpoint, since every word, every figure and every conclusion was subject to a critical review by all of these people before the survey was published.

The Statistical Background

Basic data and significant ratios were set up for ready reference in a county card file. These covered population, climate, agricultural production, industrial payrolls, forest, fish and mineral resources, land use, tax rates and public debt, and power rates. The "tooling up" period to prepare this file and the library took at least two years before any reports were written. In addition to census and trade publication data, the U. S. Forest Service, various agencies of the Department of Agriculture and the state employment services contributed considerable unpublished data.

The library also contained the major West Coast trade magazines, such as the *Pacific Fisherman* and *West Coast Lumberman* which ran many articles about individual company operations. Particularly helpful among government publications were the Forest Service surveys of the timber-producing counties which the Pacific Northwest Range and Experiment Station in Portland conducted periodically in the 1930's and 1940's. The Section also maintained a clipping file, covering not only the major Northwest newspapers but, during each survey, a representative newspaper from the county.

Statistical data provided only the skeleton; publications of other government agencies were sometimes slanted to a particular purpose; magazines and newspapers were not always accurate. But by the time we had familiarized ourselves with this background in preparation for field work, the local people were often startled by our intimate and detailed acquaintance with local business conditions, industry leaders, history, and unique features.

Another important office tool, particularly for estimating new job opportunities, was the practical industrial-engineering knowledge of the staff of the Industrial Analysis Section, twin of the Market Analysis Section in the Administration organization. Staff members of this section participated actively in the individual county surveys. An outstanding feature of each survey was their industrial pattern charts for the basic industries, which showed graphically the raw materials, primary processing plants and, at the bottom of the pyramid, the secondary processing plants in which lay the greatest job opportunities.

Trips to the county were primarily to obtain statistics about production, employment and markets that were not published and not easily obtainable by correspondence or questionnaires—from county agents, county commissioners, chambers of commerce, officials of agricultural cooperatives, owners of industrial plants.

Equally useful was the information, absorbed almost subconsciously, as to attitudes and character of business leaders and farmers. One county had an unusually active planning commission, composed of local leaders, which attempted to coordinate the public works programs of various agencies and to promote industrial and agricultural developments that would provide more jobs on a stable basis. Some businessmen were constantly looking for new products to manufacture and new markets; others were satisfied as they were or, sometimes, hopeless about the future.

When the draft of the report was completed, Bonneville staff members went back to the county to hold meetings with local people to discuss it. After these democratic free-for-all discussions, there was little danger that the final product could be accused of being an "armchair survey."

How Employment and Population Were Estimated

Subdivisions of the report followed major Census industrial employment classifications—agriculture, fishing, mining, forest industries. At the end of each subdivision were estimates of future job opportunities based on the factors brought out in the analysis.

In forest industries, potential log production of the county or its tributary area was usually the basis for job estimates. In a few counties, mill operators owned tracts in adjacent areas and this potential output could be added to the county total. Conversely, some counties would not enjoy the maximum employment possible from full utilization of their log production. The potential production figure used in most instances approximated the maximum determined by the Forest Service as allowable under sustained-yield practices; in other words, logging mature trees at a rate which would permit the younger trees to replace them, a cycle that takes at least a century. In areas that were being logged at a more rapid rate than this, the prognosis was for depletion of resources and mill shutdowns within a decade or so. However, where private owners and processors were adopting the sustained-yield principle, or where the Federal Government controlled timbered areas, actual production was likely to approximate the sustained-yield maximum, barring disastrous fires or a change in Federal policy.

According to industry experience, a certain volume of log production could employ 300 men a year; if local lumber manufacturers used all of this output, they would employ about 300 more; but if plywood mills used some of the logs, the number would be proportionately greater. Furniture manufacturing and other wood fabricating could add substantially to the number of men employed per thousand board feet; and the use of wood wastes (branches, sawdust, bark, etc.) for plastics, if carried through to fabrication stages, would add a still greater number. The probability of such developments depended as much on the ingenuity of local businessmen as on available resources and transportation facilities.

Food processing, both of farm products and of fish, offered opportunities that were just beginning to be exploited in the 1940's. Canning was an old, established industry, but quick-freezing was in its infancy. One nationally known company, started in a farmer's barn in 1936, tripled its size between 1940 and 1945. Here again, industrial experience provided ratios of the number of jobs to the volume of produce available. Seasonal peaks were being smoothed out by many companies who used a large variety of items. In the fish-processing industries especially, processors were finding markets not only for salmon and shellfish, for which the Pacific Coast already had a national reputation, but for "bottom fish" (sole, ling cod, rockfish, etc.). By-product utilization in this industry presented interesting and varied opportunities—oil for vitamin products, "shark leather" (for children's shoes), soap, synthetic pearl essence and many industrial chemicals.

Mining employment was not so readily estimated. Washington and Oregon had vast deposits of many metallic and nonmetallic minerals which the Industrial Analysis Section staff had exhaustively catalogued and appraised as to their commercial value, but transportation deficiencies and international trade uncertainties made their exploitation in the foreseeable future problematical.

Service industries appeared underdeveloped, particularly those related to the tourist trade. In estimating 1955 employment, the 1940 ratio of service to manufacturing and extractive workers (usually about eight to ten) was projected, plus in some cases a rough figure for specific developments in tourism. Furthermore, in counties with moderate-sized urban centers, this assumption seemed conservative. There was reason to expect that substantial expansion based on natural resources might be accompanied by a pyramiding of service industries in urban centers, with the ratio reaching nearly ten to ten.

The report summary brought all of the individual job estimates together. Total population was estimated by applying to total employment figures the ratio of people to jobs prevailing in 1940, a ratio which ranged from about 2.7 people per job in certain counties to about 3.3 in others. A tabulation of these estimates showed employment and total population based on development of only the more immediate opportunities and also on development of all potential opportunities. A companion tabulation listed briefly, under each major industry, group action that would expedite realization of these opportunities.

What Happened?

The 1950 Census was the first test of the job and population estimates. The 1940 Census, the estimates for 1955, and the 1950 Census, with respect to a few industries for four Washington and Oregon counties, are compared in the table on page 70. In two western Oregon counties, Coos and Linn, the 1950 census figures already exceeded the most optimistic estimates for 1955. In the other two, Skagit in northwestern Washington and Yamhill in western Oregon, the totals fell between the 1940 Census figures and the maximum estimates for 1955.

Coos and Linn Counties were heavily timbered and were among the last sources of old-growth Douglas-fir for plywood; and the migration of plywood mills and wood fabricators, already under way in the 1940's, undoubtedly accounts for most of the increase in "other" employment. Forest products industries in these counties are probably drawing on the resources of adjacent counties to a larger extent than was anticipated. Coos County especially, with an excellent harbor at Coos Bay, has become the center for the activities of one of the largest wood-using companies in the nation, which has heavy holdings throughout Southern Oregon.

Skagit and Yamhill Counties, with depleted timber resources and considerable industry based on not rapidly-expanding agricultural production, experienced more moderate growth.

Excerpts from Suggested Development Activities and Action Program for Skagit County, Washington.

	Suggested Action
I. In agricultural industries	
A. Control and development of the Skagit River	Work out a cooperative, integrated plan and encourage participation of the following agencies: U. S. Army Engineers, U. S. Soil Conservation Service, Washington State Department of Conservation and Development, board of county commissioners, Skagit County Planning Commission.
B. Land clearing	Determine suitable areas from studies by Washington State College, U. S. Soil Conservation Service, and county agricultural agent. Investigate the possibility of reducing costs by using a bulldozer co-operatively.
II. In fish industries	
A. Fishing	Urge enlargement of Federal and state fish hatcheries. Provide accommodations for larger fishing fleet at Anacortes.
B. Fish processing	Urge Washington State Department of Fisheries to assist local packers in perfecting new methods of processing and packaging and of utilizing fish wastes in the manufacture of industrial oils, medicinal preparations, etc.
III. In forest industries	
A. Plywood manufacture	Increase use of hemlock and silver fir. Investigate feasibility of making pre-fabricated plywood farm buildings designed by the U. S. Department of Agriculture.

Two other interesting points may be noted. The ratio of people to jobs was about the same in 1950 as in 1940, being something under three in both years in Coos, almost exactly three in Yamhill and Linn, and something over three in Skagit.

On the other hand, the other basic assumption, that growth in service employment would keep pace with the growth in extractive and manufacturing jobs, is not borne out by the 1950 data. The ratio of service to total employment is noticeably lower in 1950 than in 1940 in all counties except Skagit. One explanation may be that it is too early to expect the services to catch up to other industries. Much of the industrial growth did not take place until World War II ended, and the census was taken barely five years later. Coos and Linn, which had the most rapid population growth of the four counties, showed the greatest declines in the proportion of service to other workers. Apparently the greatest refinements in population-estimating techniques have still to be made in the field of service, or "non-basic," industries.

Comparison of Estimated and Actual Population and Employment Data

	Census Figures		*Estimated for 1955*	
County	1940	1950	*Minimum*	*Maximum*
Skagit — Total Pop.	37,650	43,273	39,283	49,816
Employment	11,399	13,799	11,962	15,594
Agriculture	2,691	2,389	2,811	3,041
Service	5,077	5,846	5,327	7,095
Other	3,631	5,564	3,824	5,458
Yamhill — Total Pop.	26,300	33,484	38,800	45,500
Employment	9,990	18,870	14,682	16,807
Agriculture	3,505	3,086	3,505	3,755
Service	4,062	6,679	5,999	7,092
Other	2,423	9,105	5,178	5,960
Linn — Total Pop.	30,485	54,317	44,780	51,475
Employment	11,466	16,661	11,566	13,261
Agriculture	1,535	1,219	1,535	1,695
Service	5,118	6,263	5,118	6,028
Other	4,813	9,179	4,913	5,538
Coos — Total Pop.	32,466	42,265	32,766	37,486
Employment	9,016	12,001	12,918	15,168
Agriculture	3,044	3,180	3,044	3,244
Service	3,938	4,681	6,459	7,584
Other	2,034	4,140	3,415	4,340

Ella Tambussi Grasso

CANAL FEVER: THE DEVELOPMENT OF A CONNECTICUT VALLEY TOWN

The completion of the Windsor Locks canal on November 11, 1829, marked a significant event in Connecticut River navigation. At long last, the success of river traffic was assured by this last vital link in a series of canals which made the river navigable from as far north as Wells River, Vermont, to its end at Saybrook, a distance of over 250 miles.

The shrewd Hartford merchants gathered for their noon-day meals at the Joseph Morgan Coffee House observed with more than passing interest the "canal fever" which swept the Atlantic seaboard during the decade of the 1820's. For years they had lamented the expense and inconvenience of routing their cargoes around the rapids at Enfield, in northern Connecticut, which constituted the most difficult hazard to the navigation of the Connecticut River. Mindful of the potentialities for trade with the two million inhabitants of the area, and fearful of the competition from the system of inland canals being developed by the Farmington Canal Company, they argued that more efficient utilization of the river by a series of canals to circumvent the unnavigable portions, plus use of a faster mode of transportation than sail craft, would improve and expand the river route.

In 1824 the foaming white waters of the rapids presented the same obstacle to effective use of the river as Adrian Block had encountered in his explorations two hundred years earlier. In 1641, the Dutch explorer in the *Onrust* was interrupted in his tour of the upper reaches of the river by what the Indians labeled the "white mist."

As settlements grew along the river and commerce was instituted, the rapids constituted a continuing handicap in the development of commerce in the area. William Pynchon of Agawam, later Springfield, solved the problem by building in 1636 a large warehouse at a point below the falls (later to bear the name Warehouse Point) and until the building of the bridge at Hartford in 1810 this was the head of sloop navigation. One report was that as many as sixteen sloops in one day were anchored in the river at Warehouse Point unloading products of the East and West Indian market and receiving in return the tobacco, lumber, fish and other staple exports of the area. The trip to Springfield and points north in the river was effected by portage or the use of fallsmen.

By the time of the Revolutionary War, flatboats were utilized for transportation from Hartford as far north as Wells River, Vermont. As early as 1810, regular lines of flatboats were in operation between Hartford and the towns above as far as Cheapside and Deerfield, and ten years later it is reported that some sixty scows were in operation on the river route.

A Slow and Hazardous Trip

A contemporary account describes these flatboats as from twelve to twenty tons in weight, averaging over seventy feet in length and requiring a crew of six polesmen and a captain to carry the thirty-ton loads on the river. In favorable weather, a mainsail was used, the captain steering from the stern. Usually, however, travel was slower and more laborious, as the polesmen, leaning on their stout ash poles, pushed their cargoes along.

At the falls, all cargo over twelve tons was removed and sent ahead by teams. Additional fallsmen were taken on to make the crew equal to the number of tons remaining on board, and the dangerous and skillful maneuvering along the five-mile stretch began. At the completion of the hazardous trip to the head, the fallsmen were discharged, the freight which had been sent over the old pack trails was reloaded, and the upriver journey begun. It is not surprising that the trip from Hartford to Wells, Vermont, in addition to entailing considerable expense (a dollar a day per man to get the scows over the rapids) required approximately thirty days for the round trip.

In view of the excessive costs and delays in river navigation, there is little wonder that Hartford businessmen viewed with apprehension the New Haven plan of 1822 of the Farmington Canal stockholders, which sought to divert the transportation and trade of the towns of Western Massachusetts and Eastern New York, and the states of Vermont and New Hampshire. In addition to the New Haven-Northampton route, the more elaborate plan of making connections with Lake Champlain and even extending the course into Canada presaged the emergence of New Haven not only as a competitor of Hartford but also as a rival of Boston.

Birth of the Connecticut River Company

Fortunately, in 1824, when serious consideration was given a special Connecticut River project, conditions were propitious for a favorable reception for such a program. There were signs of a business revival throughout the country, following the stagnation of the postwar period.

On January 1, 1824, a meeting of citizens to discuss "the expediency of taking measures to promote navigation of the river from this city northward" received favorable attention. Within weeks, the Connecticut River Company was organized and granted a charter by the Legislature. The charter not only provided permission to the Company to improve "the boat navigation of the Connecticut River from Hartford towards its source," but also established the corporation in the boat business by granting "the right to possess any steamboats or boats which they may judge necessary to increase transportation on said river." It also indicated the future role of the canal in industrial development by granting permission to hold or lease "mill seats or manufactories" on the locks, canals, and dams of the corporation.

A further significant development was the establishment in May 1825 of the Connecticut River Banking Company to assist in carrying out the plans of the Connecticut River Company. The report of the President that purchase of the canal properties of the upper river would entail $368,000, in addition to $1,500,000 for canal construction and improvement, made it obvious that the project was a financial undertaking of considerable magnitude.

The Memorial to the General Assembly requesting the bank was accepted over the opposition of the champions of the New Haven project and in spite of a general public mistrust of banks. The functions of the Company, however, were strictly limited by Charter, although until a few years previously little attention had been given to laws limiting a bank's operation. According to the Charter "it could purchase or hold property of whatever nature" but was forbidden to trade in anything "except bills of exchange, gold and silver bullion, or in the sale of goods pledged for money but not redeemed in due time or in lands necessarily taken for the security of debts."

The First Steamboat

While the directors surveyed the river and petitioned Congress for assistance in completing the project (an assistance which was not forthcoming), they also began investigations of the use of steam as a means of water transportation. A committee report on the use of steamboats resulted in the adoption in July 1825 of a resolution providing for the purchase or construction of a steamboat "adapted to the navigation of the Connecticut River above Hartford." On November 17, 1826, the tiny craft, 75 feet long and "14 and one-half feet beam" drawing but twenty-two inches of water without cargo reached Hartford and began its triumphal journey up the river.

Mr. Jabez Hayden in his reminiscences records the excitement caused by the appearance of the *Barnet*, as it was called. He marveled that "one man walked some distance along the shore and said the boat went as fast as he could walk"! Following some minor delays at the falls, the boat reached Springfield on November 27. Everywhere it was welcomed with enthusiasm, cannonading, receptions and jubilation. The *Boston Daily Advertiser* of December 11 hailed "the cheap, safe, regular and quick communication provided by steam navigation." The return trip of the *Barnet* to Hartford was celebrated by more oratory and festivities as the practicability and advantage of steam navigation were triumphantly demonstrated.

The success of the experiment with steam gave impetus to the actual construction of the canal at Enfield and the purchase of other canal properties northward. It was estimated that some seventeen miles of canals and forty-one locks were necessary to overcome 420 feet of descent from Barnet, Vermont, to Hartford. With the exception of the large-scale project designed for Enfield, a number of canals had already been constructed in the upper river. In 1795 the Proprietors of the Locks and Canals on the Connecticut River, chartered by Massachusetts, completed the construction of locks and canals at South Hadley. It is understood that this project was made so attractive that a considerable portion of the capitalization was obtained from Holland. It is of interest to note that instead of the ordinary method of raising vessels by locks to a higher level, an inclined plane was devised, which apparently worked satisfactorily. The canal at Turners Falls was opened in 1800, the one at Bellows Falls in 1802, and later two small canals further north completed the upper Connecticut route.

The Canal at Enfield

Construction of the Enfield canal began in earnest in the early summer of 1827, as Irish workmen were imported to dig the long and difficult trench. The descent of some four hundred Irishmen on the Pinemeadow (later Windsor Locks) community must have caused a considerable stir, one worldly diarist recording "the digging of the canal was done by Irishmen who came here for the purpose. I remember having seen but one before."

The canal, which for some distance marks the eastern bounds of Windsor Locks, was six miles in length, extending from Pinemeadow to Suffield. The *Connecticut Mirror* of November 16, 1829, reported: "the breadth and depth are such as to admit not only the ordinary flat bottomed boats used on the river, but steam boats of much larger draught." Engineers have estimated "breadth and depth" as about 80′ and 4½′ in the open section with locks 18′ wide and 90′ long in the clear. Three locks at the lower end of the falls, of about ten feet lift each, were constructed of stone laid in water cement. Another lock was built at the head of the canal together with a massive breast wall. It is believed that the locks are probably duplicates of the all-masonry locks of the Farmington canal. The aquaduct over Stony Brook, which is still in use, is 104 feet long overall, in five spans carried by the two abutments and four piers. The trough consists of a series of large logs parallel to the canal and lined with planks.

The completion of the project two years later was celebrated on November 11, 1829, with the passage of fifteen boats through the new canal, the trip, including lockage time, requiring between an hour and an hour and a half. While the Irish workmen lined the banks and cheered, the stockholders in Thomas Blanchard's newly-invented stern-wheel steamer toured the area, surveying the dual results of their investments in transportation.

Until the inauguration of regular railroad service in 1844, a large number of up-river scow-boats passed through the canal. John Warner Barber in 1836 records that "8 steamboats, including four passengers ply daily between Hartford and Springfield." Six of these were used as tow boats.

Charles Dickens, who made the canal trip in 1844, immortalized the canal in his *American Notes,* estimating the speed at "half-a-pony power," adding, "Mr. Paap, the celebrated dwarf, might have lived and died happily in the cabin."

The demise of the canal as a means of transportation with the coming of the Railroad was also a prelude to extensive activity for manufacturing purposes. Mill owners purchased water from the Connecticut River Company and leased land on which to build their factories.

Uses of Water Power

The first water power drawn from the canal was used by a gin distillery, erected in 1811, and previously operated by water from a pond where the canal now exists. During the period of great activity on the canal only a small part of the water power was taken. In 1846, a new departure by the Company, obviously in search of revenues to augment dwindling toll receipts, resulted in the granting of leases at reduced prices. This not only proved an impetus to manufacturing but also established the Pinemeadow as an integral community, so that in 1854 it was incorporated as the township of Windsor Locks.

For some time the main product of the mills along the canal bank was paper, first begun in 1838. By 1857 Persse and Brooks operated the largest paper mills in the world at Windsor Locks.

A. Bristol, a Windsor Locks historian, reports that by 1909 there were twelve manufacturing plants along the canal bank making all kinds of paper products, spool silk, woolen goods, chucks, hand trucks, casters, cutlery, cotton goods, electricity and other items. To meet the requirements of a changing economy these consumer products have since been augmented by such items as filter paper, lens polishers, tinsel, wire, combination lawn mower and snow removal equipment, diesel engine valve gauges and patented jet aircraft fuel tank covers.

The canal, which contributed to the expansion of business activity in the upper-river towns, is used now chiefly as a source of water power for the factories lining its banks. With the decline of water transportation, activity on the canal has been limited to an occasional pleasure craft.

Yet, in its heyday the canal brought pleasure and prosperity to a large section of the Connecticut Valley. It was responsible for the development of the town of Windsor Locks and continues as a source of water power to serve a vital role in its economy.

Louise Pearson Mitchell

ALEXANDER HAMILTON AS A LIEUTENANT OF ROBERT MORRIS

For nearly the whole of Alexander Hamilton's conspicuous and well-known public service as Secretary of the Treasury, the materials are to be found in his earlier experiences, either in the Revolution itself or in the confused and trying period of the Confederation. In no case is this more clearly seen than in the few months during 1782 when, on appointment by Robert Morris, Hamilton was Continental Receiver of Taxes for New York State.

On February 20, 1781, Morris was, by unanimous vote of Congress, elected to the new office of Superintendent of Finance (replacing the old, inefficient ten-member Treasury Board). After some months of negotiation, in which he successfully insisted on the right of appointment of all personnel of his department, Morris accepted the responsibility on May 14, 1781. Hamilton, although mentioned himself at least once for this post, had months earlier spoken of Morris as the suitable person. In a letter to James Duane, dated September 3, 1780, Hamilton set forth at length his ideas of the shortcomings of the system of government. He said that Congress should appoint "great officers of State" for various departments, choosing for them "men of the first abilities, property, and character, in the Continent; and such as have had the best opportunities of being acquainted with the several branches . . . Mr. Robert Morris would have many things in his favor for the department of finance. He could, by his personal influence, give great weight to the measures he should adopt."

Hamilton also, in a letter of April 30, 1781, expressed to

Morris his warm approval of the appointment: "I know of no other in America, who unites so many advantages; and of course every impediment to your acceptance, is to me a subject of chagrin . . . as one deeply interested in the event, I am happy in believing you will not easily be discouraged from undertaking an office, by which you may render America, and the world, no less a service than the establishment of American independence. 'Tis by introducing order into our finances by restoring public credit—not by gaining battles, that we are finally to gain our object . . . . In the frankness of truth I believe, sir, you are the man best capable of performing this great work."

Difficulties of Collecting Taxes

When Morris accepted his office, the Articles of Confederation had only just been finally ratified by the last state. It was not yet fully realized, therefore, how ineffectual the scheme was to prove, notably of course as to taxation. The thirteen states were supposed to provide the main source of the income Morris must secure for the successful prosecution of the war, and to that end Morris had to work with the several state legislatures. The frustration and futility of this can hardly be imagined; Morris said it was "like preaching to the dead." Every possible device of persuasion, cajolery and threat was used in the effort to get the states to play their proper part in financing the war.

One of Morris's plans was to replace the loan officers, appointed by Congress early in the war, with a carefully-chosen Receiver of Continental Taxes for each state. These loan officers, negotiating domestic loans, had issued for them interest-bearing certificates. If the interest could not be paid in money (the almost universal predicament), new certificates were granted instead. Opposed to such financial methods, Morris wrote the loan officers soon after his appointment, telling them of his intention to reorganize the Treasury Department and use others for tax collection. Congress, by an act of November 2, 1781, gave him authority to appoint either the loan officer in each state, or some other person, to receive the taxes requested by the national government.

It was under this authority that Morris appointed Hamilton to the post of Receiver for the State of New York, in a letter of May 2, 1782. Hamilton at first was not inclined to accept; his objections were that he was engaged in the study of law, and wanted to qualify promptly, and that the post offered would pay less than enough to be worth his diverting himself (May 18, 1782). Morris sought to reassure him on both counts. The rate offered, one-fourth of one per cent, was to be paid on the whole of the state's quota ($373,598), even if the entire sum were not collected; "consequently the object is greater than you supposed, and the business might probably be effected without more attention than you would spare from your studies." (June 4, 1782).

This time Hamilton accepted (June 17, 1782) but now wondered whether "the service I can render, in the present state of things, will be equivalent for the compensation." It seemed to him that there was little for a Continental Receiver of Taxes to do. He asked for Morris's orders, since the Legislature was due to convene the following month. The gratified reply, asking Hamilton to proceed at once with the task of persuading the Legislature to allocate a share of taxes to Continental use, set forth also Morris's reasons for his choice of the younger man (July 2, 1782): "Your former situation in the army, the present situation of that very army, your connections in the State, your perfect knowledge of men and measures, and the abilities which heaven has blessed you with, will give you a fine opportunity to forward the public service. . . ."

Hamilton at once set about informing himself for his task. He wrote to William Duer and to Comfort Sands, both of whom had been concerned in provisioning the army, asking them for estimates of disbursements for army supplies in New York State for a year. By mid-July, 1782, he set out for Poughkeepsie and the special session of the Legislature, convened by Governor Clinton to confer with a Congressional committee "on the Necessity of providing competent Means for a vigorous Prosecution of the War." This sounded promising, but Hamilton was not sanguine of much result. The last preceding session of the Legislature, urgently called for the same reasons, had failed to aid the Continental cause.

His warrant as Receiver promptly submitted to Governor Clinton, Hamilton at the same time asked for a conference with a joint legislative committee, that he might convey to it Morris's views and the urgency of the situation. In a letter to Morris (July 22, 1782), he reported progress: "I strongly represented [to the legislative commitee] the necessity of solid arrangements of finance, and, by way of argument, pointed out all the defects of the present system. I found every man convinced that something was wrong, but few that were willing to recognize the mischief when defined, and consent to the proper remedy. . . . a bill has . . passed both Houses, payable in specie, bank notes, or your notes, for eighteen thousand pounds. It is at present appropriated to your order, but I doubt whether some subsequent arrangement will not take place for a different appropriation. The Commander-in-Chief has applied for a quantity of forage, which the Legislature is devising the means of furnishing, and I fear it will finish by diverting the eighteen thousand pounds to that purpose. I have hitherto been able to prevent this, but as it is of indispensable importance to me to leave this place immediately to prepare for my examination. . . it is possible, after I have left it, that contrary ideas will prevail. . . . Should the bill for the eighteen thousand pounds go out in its present form, I cannot hope that it will produce in the treasury above half the sum, such are the vices of our present mode of collection."

In the same letter, Hamilton mentioned two other actions of the New York Legislature having far more significance than the immediate fate of the eighteen-thousand pounds appropriation and whether or not it was diverted to payment in kind as forage. One was the appointment of a committee to devise a better scheme of taxation for the State, during the Legislature's recess, in consultation with Hamilton. He was, he said, "Convinced of the absurdity of multiplying taxes in the present mode, where, in effect, the payment is voluntary, and the money received exhausted in the collection. . ."; hence he was urging a real change in plan, and believed that truth was "making some progress."

Call for a Constitutional Convention

The other development, even more far-reaching in its ultimate consequence, was the work of Hamilton and Philip Schuyler, his father-in-law, together. They had found the invariable answer, if reforms were urged, was "What avails it for one State to make them without the concert of the others?" In the conviction that only thorough-going political reforms would solve the problem, country-wide, they secured the passage by the New York Legislature of what amounted to a call for a constitutional convention. Nine resolutions, proposed by Schuyler in the Senate, passed there and concurred in by the House, were based on a full consideration of the state of affairs, domestic and foreign. The plan of Congress for the finances was declared to be "founded in Wisdom and sound Policy, and. . . . A Failure in this System, for Want of the Support which the States are able to give, would be productive of Evils too pernicious to be hazarded." It was further "Resolved, That . . . the radical Source of most of our Embarrassments, is the Want of Sufficient Power in Congress."

The final conviction was that the repair of national credit and a successful conclusion of the war "can never be attained by partial deliberations of the States separately; but that it is essential to the common Welfare, that there should be as soon as possible a Conference of the Whole on the Subject; and that it would be adviseable for this Purpose, to propose to Congress to recommend, and to each State to adopt the Measure of, assembling a general Convention of the States, especially authorized to revise and amend the Confederation, reserving a Right to the respective Legislatures to ratify their Determinations."

This was the first call by a public body, anticipating the meeting at Mount Vernon and the Annapolis and Philadelphia conventions, looking toward the establishment of the Federal Constitution. Hamilton, however, despite his warm advocacy of such a step and the deep conviction of its necessity, was not hopeful of its success at that time. His letter to Morris of July 22, written two days after the passage of the resolution, says that he considers this proposed convention of the states "a very eligible step, though I doubt of the concurrence of the other States; but I am certain without it they will never be brought to co-operate in any reasonable or effectual plan."

Hamilton Elected to Congress

On the same day that his long letter of report to Morris was written, Hamilton was elected to Congress by the New York Legislature. His term would begin in November, which would then remove him from the office of Continental Receiver; in Congress, however, he would be in a better position to urge the political reforms necessary to satisfactory revenue. In writing to Colonel Richard Meade, his former fellow-aide, Hamilton said of his election, "I do not hope to reform the State, although I shall endeavor to do all the good I can."

Meanwhile, however, Hamilton exerted himself in every possible way to fulfill his promises and obligations to Morris in his present post. Early in August, he applied to Governor Clinton for the complete and specific financial information as to New York State, back to March, 1780, requested by Morris in July,

1781. At the same time, he wrote to all the County Treasurers, asking for information as to tax receipts and the cost of collection, for the same period. He had already requested W. E. Bancker, the State Treasurer, to remit the overdue first payment on New York's quota, and to collect more promptly in the future.

New York Situation Described

Pending replies to these inquiries, Hamilton sent Morris on August 13 a long review of the general situation in New York, as he had promised. Beginning with an estimate of the damage inflicted on the State during the war, and changes in population, his conclusion is that its tax resources "are diminished at least two thirds." New York's exertions in the war were great, indeed often "of the most exhausting kind," although perhaps less efficiently rendered than might have been ideal. Expenditures for the army in specie, "or such paper as answers the purpose of specie," might have totalled $180,000, but this was more than outweighed by purchases from other states. This unfavorable balance of trade left *"an extreme* and *universal* scarcity of money."

As to the State's government, here was found "the general disease which infects all our Constitutions—an excess of popularity. . . . The inquiry constantly is what will *please,* not what will *benefit* the people." As to assessment and taxation of property, influence and privilege figured much more largely than equity or ability to pay. The system, although "iniquitous and fruitless," cannot be amended "without totally changing it. . . ." Although the political leaders were attached to the Patriot cause, he estimated one-third of the people's "secret wishes are on the side of the enemy; the remainder sigh for peace, murmur at taxes, clamor at their rulers, change one incapable man for another more incapable, and, I fear, if left to themselves would, too many of them, be willing to purchase peace at any price—not from inclination to Great Britain or disaffection to independence, but from mere supineness and avarice." Supposing the Legislature willing to adopt a better tax system, about £40,000 might be available for Continental purposes; failing such change, about one-third of that sum.

Although he has "neither flattered the State nor encouraged high expectations," he will "strive to convince the committee, when they meet, that a change of measures is essential; if they enter cordially into right views, we may succeed; but I confess I fear more than I hope."

Similarity of Thinking

A long reply to this and earlier communications, dated August 28, 1782, reveals the similarity of Hamilton's and Morris' thinking. Referring to the Legislature's resolutions of July 20, Morris said, "A firm, wise, manly system of federal government is what I once wished, what I now hope, what I dare not expect, but what I will not despair of." His reception of the description of tax collection in New York is sympathetic: "There is no end to the absurdity of human nature. Mankind seem to delight in contrast and paradox; for surely nothing else could sanctify (during a contest on the precise point of being taxed by our own consent) the arbitrary policy which, on this subject, almost universally prevails. God grant you success in your views to amend it." As to the review of the New York situation, "The account you give of the State is by no means flattering: and the more true it appears, the more concern it gives me. The loan, I hope, will be completed; and I wish the *whole* amount of the tax may be collected."

Morris demurs, however, at the degree of exhaustion pictured by Hamilton, "The scarcity of money. . . may be immediately relieved, if the love of popular favor would so far give way to the love of public good, as to enforce plentiful taxation. The necessity of having money will always produce money. The desire of having it, produces, you see, so much as is necessary to gratify the desire of enjoying foreign luxuries. Turn the stream, which now flows in the channels of Commerce, to those of Revenue, and the business is completed. Unfortunately for us, this is an operation which requires fortitude, perseverance, virtue; and which cannot be effected by the weak or wicked minds who have only partial, private or interested views." In spite of his realism, the older man is mellower and more hopeful than Hamilton: "When I consider the exertions which the country you possess has already made, under striking disadvantages, and with astonishing prodigality of national wealth, by pernicious modes of applying it; I persuade myself, that regular, consistent efforts, would produce much more than you suppose."

The correspondence between Hamilton and Morris shows, in general, remarkable like-mindedness. Technical differences there were, however, at a number of points. These may be illustrated by a letter of Hamilton dated September 21, 1782. He suggests that Morris' Continental notes, although "in credit with the merchants by way of remittance," do not circulate as freely as would be desirable. Not issued in denominations smaller than $20, Hamilton believes that their size makes them inconvenient even for paying taxes, and he suggests issuing them in denominations of five, eight or ten dollars.

This suggestion, although easily understandable because of the continual anxiety for abundant circulating media, was rejected by Morris in a letter of October 5. His explanations are tactful, but firm, making first the observation that "Confidence is a plant of very slow growth; and our political situation is not too favorable to it." The large denominations were deliberate; mercantile people would find them convenient to their uses, and more likely to accept them. "Whenever the shopkeepers, in general, discover that my paper will answer as a remittance to the principal ports, and will be readily exchanged by the Receivers, they will as readily exchange it for other people. When the people, in general, find that the shopkeepers receive it freely, they will begin to look after it, and not before. . . . the farmers will not give full credit to money, merely because it will pay taxes; for that is an object they are not very violently devoted to. But that money which goes freely at the store and the tavern, will be sought after as greedily as those things which the store and the tavern contain." Acknowledging that twenty dollars is not a convenient denomination, Morris goes further: ". . . there is infinitely less danger that large notes, which go only through the hands of intelligent people, will be counterfeited than small ones, which come to the possession of illiterate men. When public credit is firmly established, the little shocks it receives from the counterfeiters of paper money, do not lead to material consequences; but, in the present ticklish state of things, there is just ground of apprehension. Besides this, the value of paper will depend much upon the interchange of it for specie; and these will not take place when there is a circulation of small paper."

Hamilton accepted Morris' kindly correction with good grace, on the whole, although he says, in a letter of October 26, that some of the "very cogent reasons" had occurred to him independently. "While I acknowledge that your observations have corrected my ideas upon the subject, and shown me that there would be danger in generally lessening the denominations of the paper issued, I should be uncandid not to add that it still appears to me there would be a preponderance of advantages in having a *part* of a smaller amount."

Partial Success

Meanwhile the committee of the Legislature on tax measures had met. In a letter of September 28, Hamilton wrote Morris rather disparagingly: "The committee on the subject of taxation are met. Some have their plans, and they must protect their own children, however misshapen; others have not, but are determined to find fault with all. I expect little, but I shall promote any thing, though imperfect, that will mend our situation."

On October 5 the results of the committee's deliberations were reported. Evidently Hamilton tried hard to get a comprehensive program adopted, with only partial success. "In spite of my efforts, they have parted without doing anything decisive. They have, indeed, agreed upon several matters, and these of importance, but they have not reduced them to the form of a report, which, in fact, leaves everything afloat, to be governed by the impressions of the moment when the Legislature meets." In general, the committee's conclusions were much less specific and carefully calculated than were Hamilton's proposals to it. He must have felt, in spite of discouragement, that his efforts had borne some fruit. Among the points of agreement were a tax on personal property, luxury taxes on such articles as watches, clocks and carriages, a poll-tax on single men, taxes on money "at usury" except loans to the public, houses in towns to be taxed at a proportion of the annual rent. He speaks regretfully of losing a proposal for "an excise on distilled liquors, but all that could be carried on this article was a license on taverns." Funding was considered indispensable for paying old debts and procuring further credit, but such provision by New York alone was not approved.

Ability to Look Ahead

In his post of Continental Receiver, Hamilton's mind constantly leapt from the practical impasse of the moment to more hopeful, thorough remedies. The suspension of interest payment on the loan certificates, early in the Revolution, produced distress and discontent among the holders. Earlier in 1782, a meeting of these creditors was held in Philadelphia, which made Hamilton think possibly a concerted demand from all over the country for restoration of Continental credit might provide the lever necessary for a new Federal Constitution. Accordingly, a meeting was held at Albany in September, presided over by General Schuyler. A state convention of county delegates, to be held at Poughkeepsie, was proposed, and a state delegation to a general convention at Philadelphia, in an address "To the Public Creditors of the State of New York."

Although the tone of this address, composed by Hamilton, was persuasive rather than peremptory, it was a bold and risky move. If public creditors were brought together to exert pressure on States and Confederations, the results might well be to increase disgruntlement and disaffection. Apparently this Albany meeting had no direct consequences; Hamilton's part in it (like his later momentary notion of using the unpaid army to coerce Congress) best illustrate the urgency of his feeling that political reform took precedence over other problems.

On October 31, 1782, Hamilton resigned his office under Morris, as he was shortly to set out for Philadelphia and his duties in Congress. He was succeeded as Receiver by Dr. William Tillotson. The whole episode covered no more than five months, during which Hamilton was also occupied in the important matter of qualifying as attorney and counsellor-at-law. Yet we find abundantly demonstrated his energy in the public service, his debt to the foremost financial intelligence of the Revolution, the breadth and detail of his own grasp. Even more fundamental to Hamilton's thinking was the way in which his experiences, at every turn, reinforced the conclusion that the new nation must give the central government greater power if it were to survive.

Finally, it requires no exercise of the imagination to conclude that here Hamilton was assisted greatly in the ultimate formulation of the plans he submitted to Congress as our first Secretary of the Treasury.

Bibliography

Hamilton, John C., ed.: *The Works of Alexander Hamilton*, John F. Trow, Printer, New York, Vol. I, 1850.

Hamilton, John C.: *History of the Republic of the United States of America. . . .* , D. Appleton & Co., New York, Vol. II, 1858.

Lodge, Henry Cabot, ed.: *The Works of Alexander Hamilton,* Federal Edition, G. P. Putnam's Sons, New York and London, Vol. IX, 1904.

Sparks, Jared: *The Diplomatic Correspondence of the American Revolution.* John C. Rives, pub., Washington, D. C., Vol. VI, 1857.

Votes and Proceedings of the Senate of the State of New York, Vol. II, 1782.

Hamilton MSS., Library of Congress, Vol. IV, No. 433.

Edith Hyslop Sherrard

ECONOMIC HISTORY RECONSIDERED: A BACKWARD GLANCE AT THE STUDY OF HUSBANDRY AND CRAFT

In the last analysis, what one gets out of any course in college is a purely personal affair; and even then, the extent of this harvest—of this winnowing, to be more accurate—may not be revealed for years. In retrospect one may find that Statistics was the foundation stone of a profitable career. Or that Philosophy or English Literature or Economic and Social History provided a point of view which has weathered the test of time rather well. Or one may find that one got nothing out of the course, except possibly an "A" which now, like a faded laurel wreath, has only a sentimental value.

For some of us economic history was, at the time, a personal experience. It was my exploration of the way the people of a nation lived—lived in the most physical sense of the word. It opened out before me then, and comes back to me now, as a continuity of amazingly sensatory experiences. In short, it conveyed the complex of things in which each man must live in his own time: Flora and fauna—food, pasture, and trees; livestock, quartered with the family perhaps, in a single room. A condition of housing—the damp cold of stone, or the smells of woods of one sort or another. A condition of health—hazards of infancy, of crippling diseases or deformities, and the thousand marks of household accidents. A condition of clothing—coarse or elegant, severe or ceremonial; always rather hardwearing. A condition of labor—handicraft or factory; trades practiced as one's own master, or within the guild, or under the shop steward. One's view of oneself—the child of God, the warrior against nature, the lonely defendant in a never-ending combat against accident, thieves, stern justice, and disease. Relationships with others—the warmth of society, duties given and taken, recognized authorities spiritual and temporal.

I must say the instructors and the bibliographies did well in satisfying this particular taste for knowledge. Years later, when first I saw France and England, I was convinced that their flavor was authentic!

The Approach to Reality

In a sense this personal kind of study of history is a quest, and a quest that recognizes the perpetual elusiveness of the goal. What *was* life like in seventeenth and eighteenth century England, we ask? We begin to collect facts and recreate the man. We study clothing and housing and look up statistics. We tabulate attitudes—toward God, country, wife and child. We observe the consumption of beer, and note that "beer" then meant something heavier (or lighter) than mild-and-bitter does now. Closer and closer to the reality we come. And then, in a moment, the picture is cast in doubt by Virginia Woolf who suggests (it does not matter how seriously) that the weather in the seventeenth and eighteenth centuries was different from the weather now. Beer is one thing—but weather! Let her describe its ubiquity: After the first day of the nineteenth century, she writes in *Orlando,*

> Rain fell frequently . . . The sun shone of course, but it was so girt about with clouds and the air was so saturated with water, that its beams were discolored and purples, oranges, and reds of a dull sort took the place of the more positive landscapes of the eighteenth century . . . But what was worse, damp now began to make its way into every house . . . Damp swells the wood, furs the kettle, rusts the iron, rots the stone . . . Thus, stealthily and imperceptibly, none marking the exact day or hour of the change, the constitution of England was altered and nobody knew it . . . The hardy country gentleman, who had sat down gladly to a meal of ale and beef in a room designed, perhaps by the brothers Adam, with classic dignity, now felt chilly. Rugs appeared; beards were grown; trousers were fastened tight under the instep. The chill which he felt in his legs the country gentleman soon transferred to his house; furniture was muffled; walls and tables were covered; nothing was left bare.

If this is what happened to England in the nineteenth century how can we know what England was like before that? After we know everything that the record shows, how can we be sure we know anything? To the list above, we must now add *Weather*—heat and cold, sun and rain, and the degree of exposure to them.

A certain agility of mind is required, it seems. First, we must develop a nose for reality, like a bird dog. And at the same time we must learn to recognize and resist our own preconceptions; we must acquire a nice sense of humility about our capacity for understanding anything that is not part of our own experience, and a sense of wariness about projecting our own experience upon the lives of other folk. (An odd sister in the family of social sciences, this economic history!)

Few of us succeed in acquiring more than a respect for this agility of mind; but some, who have attained the quality itself, not only demonstrate once more that scholarship may be its own reward but even point a simple moral for those who would dabble in human relations. To borrow from the experience of a classical scholar, Edith Hamilton (in *The Greek Way*) got more nearly within the mind of another people than most of us get within their own:

> In Egypt the centre of interest was the dead. The ruling world power, a splendid empire—and death a foremost preoccupation. Countless numbers of human beings for countless numbers of centuries thought of death as that which was nearest and most familiar to them. It is an extraordinary circumstance which could be made credible by nothing less considerable than the immense mass of Egyptian art centered in the dead. To the Egyptian the enduring world of reality was not the one he walked in along the paths of every-day life but the one he should presently go to by the way of death.

And of Greece, by contrast, she says:

> The Greeks were the first people in the world to play, and they played on a great scale. All over Greece there were games, all sorts of games; athletic contests of every description: races—horse-, boat-, foot-, torch-races; contests in music, where one side outsung the other; in dancing—on greased skins sometimes to display a nice skill of foot and balance of body; games where men leaped in and out of flying chariots; games so many one grows weary with the list of them. . . . If we had no other knowledge of what the Greeks were like, if nothing were left of Greek art and literature, the fact that they were in love with play and played magnificently would be proof enough of how they lived and how they looked at life. Wretched people, toiling people, do not play. Nothing like the Greek games is conceivable in Egypt or Mesopotamia.

The twentieth century western mind does not contemplate death in the same way as the ancient Egyptian mind; and it may be true, as some have suggested, that we try to obscure and disguise its significance. Now, if the contemporary scholar of Egyptian history were bound by our view of death, how could she have interpreted "the immense mass of Egyptian art centered in the dead"? As evidence only of an upper class of great wealth and of a most unequal distribution of income? How inadequate—and even unreal—from the Egyptian point of view!

It seems odd that one might acquire a nose for reality as a result of contemplating the life of the ancient Greeks—or, for that matter, life on the American frontier. Yet, since things-past do not fit easily into any preconception of how they ought to be, we are forced to look at them fully and roundly. Contemporary affairs do not seem to sharpen the powers of observation in the same way, except occasionally when some shocking event requires us to look at the facts—and not only to have views about them.

Eileen Power stands out in my memory of economic history as a shining exponent of a vivid and personal approach to the way people live; and she, if anyone, had a strong sense of reality to guide her. In "The Menagier's Wife," a chapter of *Medieval People,* she describes a book written by a fourteenth century burgess of Paris for the instruction of his young wife. Here the gentleman enumerated the qualities and skills he found most commendable in a wife—and his recipes for attaining them. No topic was too small for his attention, no instruction too specific, no circumstance too unpredictable. His choice of qualities in a wife conveys a view of the world quite alien from our own, yet perfectly consistent and viable. The burgess likens ". . . the wife's love for her husband to the fidelity of domestic animals towards their masters." But he is tender towards her, and sympathetic to her pride:

> In his Prologue, addressed to her, he gives a charming picture of the scene which led him to write his book: "You, being of the age of fifteen years and in the week that you and I were wed, did pray me that I would please to be indulgent to your youth and to your small and ignorant service mewards, . . . praying me humbly . . . that for the love of God I would not correct you harshly before strangers nor before our own folk, but that I would correct you each night or from day to day in our chamber . . . And I thought well of, and praise and thank you for, what you said to me and I have often remembered it since.

The burgess of Paris would have been puzzled (as well as shocked!) by the proposed Equal Rights Amendment to the Constitution of the United States. Why *equal* rights, he would wonder? Why not rights for men and rights for women—duties given and taken? He himself has a strong sense of responsibility for his wife's welfare which he reveals in an odd little way:

> He is old, he says, and must die before her, and it is positively essential that she should do him credit with her second husband. What a reflection upon him if she accompanied his successor to Mass with the collar of her *cotte* crumpled, or if she knew not how to keep fleas from the blankets, or how to order a supper for twelve in Lent!

There is more than one view of husband-and-wife, it seems. There is more than one view of death. And these views are perfectly consistent and workable within their own societies. We may "come back" from medieval England or Paris in the fourteenth century with a strong sense that we prefer our own arrangements. Yet we cannot help but see them thereafter with a little more perspective—see them, that is, in their strengths and in their weaknesses.

The context of economic history pertains to all men, not only to men who have had greatness thrust upon them; and it pertains to them continuously in the act of making a living. As we explore ways of life that preceded our own, we cannot help but develop a point of view: The individual is surprisingly tough and resilient and weathers an amazing amount of buffeting about, we may note, but society seems to be a much more fragile arrangement. The individual can stand a high degree of strain and tension, but the group may be threatened more seriously by these than by dangers that require heroic action. The consequences of social action are likely to be unpredictable because men are, after all, individuals and do not always act as they are "supposed" to. In short, it is dangerous to generalize about men and affairs unless one has a strong grip on reality.

The Retreat From Reality?

Few people would argue with these conclusions as they relate to the past. Yet we seem to change our standards quickly when we look at ourselves and our own situation. A certain boldness characterizes many of our propositions. Far from being impressed with the fragility of society, we constantly poke and prod at it. Feeling quite sure about what people want (or ought to want) we are willing to define socially desirable goals in a wide range of human relationships.

If this is not already the age of social science, it is certainly the hour before the dawn. But at the very moment when a counsel of caution—such a counsel as economic history provides—would seem to be the indispensable element in applied social science, many practitioners of the art operate on quite opposite assumptions.

In the United States, the tide runs in the direction of social engineering, and it is reinforced by certain attributes of the national character. A feeling of optimism about "progress," an impatience with delay and complexity, and a fairly persistent unwillingness to let one another alone—all these combine to bring the practitioner and his clientele together in the common pursuit of problem-solving and self-improvement.

This will go on, and perhaps not too much damage will be done. (The individual, we have said, is resilient.) In any event I do not propose to quarrel with manifest destiny. But it does seem that the student of social science has a responsibility to watch out for secondary developments in the wake of his reforms; and one ominous development already demands attention. As I work with an adult education program in social studies, the impression grows on me that our apprehension of reality is becoming increasingly vague. Since it is our purpose in social science to talk about complex material in terms of generalities, *no thing* is ever seen fully and roundly. We cannot always tell where one problem begins and where another ends. We talk of human relations as if they were abstractions; and we do not seem concerned about the "who" who practices them. I believe that some of Kinsey's critics are fumbling around for words to make just this complaint about his statistical picture of *Sexual Behavior in the Human Female.*

I do not mean to propose that social science has caused us to lose our grip on reality—certainly not by itself anyway. But I do believe that the habit of generalizing about cause and effect and life at large aggravates such a tendency—particularly when, as we have noted, the untrained client is invited to join the practitioner in his art. What is more, I think social science has an interest in resisting this tendency toward vagueness.

In the last analysis, generalizations are supposed to be accurate; descriptions that do not describe are no help to the profession. As a composite example of just such a description we might consider quotations from two little pamphlets designed to acquaint foreigners with life in the United States. The first of these, written a few years ago and distributed by the United States Information Service, tells us:

> There are 550 symphony orchestras in the United States. The 25 largest professional symphony orchestras employ 80 to 110 musicians each. Together, these 550 orchestras give more than 10,000 concerts during each music season. (*Facts About the United States.* Distributed by the United States Information Service, 1951.)

Just think of it: 550 symphony orchestras—each one of them either good or bad or indifferent! One can almost see the emigrants crowding the distant shore in their eagerness to be off. But this is not all; other surprises await them. Our second pamphlet tells us:

> "Dating" is an American custom not practiced in some parts of the world. A man may invite a woman to go out with him socially when they enjoy each other's company. This makes it possible for them to know each other better and provides increasing opportunities for men and women to understand each other's interests and points of view. (*An Introduction to the United States of America—For the Visitor From Abroad.* Prepared by the Young Adult Council of the National Social Welfare Assembly, revised, 1952.)

Dating, I feel obliged to say, provides other opportunities too—at least in certain parts of the United States.

Just as one can develop a nose for reality in certain circumstances, one can fail, it seems, to develop a nose for reality in other circumstances. In fact, one can quite lose touch with reality; and this in the age of social science would be a disaster.

Social scientists today need more training in economic history, not less; and their study of it must be a personal experience, each student carrying on his own exploration of the way a people live. For the more we devise broad principles about human behavior, the more we must remind ourselves that experience is apprehended by a single brain, that life is lived by individuals. Somehow we must learn to see men as they see themselves—to see them in their importance, and not just to measure them.

Hamilton, Edith: *The Greek Way,* W. W. Norton & Co., New York, 1948.

Power, Eileen: *Medieval People,* Methuen & Co., Ltd., London, 1924.

Woolf, Virginia: *Orlando,* Penguin Books edition, New York, 1946, reprinted by permission of Harcourt, Brace & Co., Inc.

Carolyn Shaw Bell

INNOVATION AND CONSUMPTION

In the American economy technological change and innovation are at once familiar characteristics and unknown quantities. To the businessman, new products or processes may result in great profits or losses; he cannot afford to be unaware of them. To the economist, the whole process of innovation makes our country dynamic rather than stable. Capitalism has been identified with innovation and its "creative destruction" of jobs, firms, and industries which give way to new jobs, firms, and industries.

For the most part, however, we think of technological change primarily in terms of production. Both business cycles and economic development have been explained in terms of innovation—new production functions—within the firm, with repercussions on competing firms and in the economy as a whole. Innovation and production are associated in popular opinion as well, where the bogey of technological unemployment continually recurs, along with the equally dire and overemphasized suspicion that large firms suppress patents. By and large, the effects of innovation on consumption have not been investigated, for reasons which will appear in this article.

One narrow view is that consumer tastes and preferences, which (with income) determine what goods are bought and used, lie outside the range of economics. "A comprehensive theory of consumer preferences must rest on the laws of formation and structure of social cultures. The discovery of these laws is the enviable task of social anthropology, and the economist *qua* economist can render only modest assistance in this important work." (Stigler, *Theory of Competitive Price.*) The economist is, however, a student of business enterprise, and much enterprise is devoted to forming, or attempting to form, consumer tastes. We can scarcely relegate the whole field of advertising and merchandising to social anthropology, although certain of its customs, totems and taboos might well be viewed in this light. More importantly, when firms introduce innovation, consumption is directly affected.

It is the thesis of this article that the role of innovation in the economy has a two-fold effect on consumer tastes and preferences: that innovation has not only increased the range and variety of choices available to consumers, but that innovation has itself come to form a distinct part of what consumers buy.

Income as a Determinant of Consumption

Most explanations of consumption single out income as the dominant influence. Purchases of goods and services run into more money among higher-income families than among lower-income families, but the relatively well-off spend less, as a proportion of their incomes, than do the relatively poor. The excess income, of course, goes into savings for the well-to-do, while at low income levels savings may be very small or non-existent.

But this analysis holds only for a given population at a given point in time. Since 1900 incomes as a whole have increased markedly, yet consumption as a whole has increased too, rather than taking a smaller proportion of the new, higher income. In explaining this apparent paradox, the best-known solution is that of James Deusenberry, in *Income, Saving, and the Theory of Consumer Behavior* (Harvard Economic Studies, 1949). The author suggests that consumption choices are interdependent, and reflect not money income but the relative position of the family in the income distribution. Then, as income increases, consumption expenditures increase in order to maintain the same place or rank among all the families with increased incomes. Spending increases in the purchase of more goods and better quality goods, things already familiar to any consumer from the way of life of those just above him in the income scale.

This general progression to a higher standard of living depends, Mr. Deusenberry maintains, on general agreement as to what constitutes better quality in cars and furniture and appliances and clothing and education. The drive to acquire a higher standard of living seems a deep-seated national characteristic, which perhaps should be explained by the cultural and social psychologists.

What seems lacking from the entire emphasis on income as a

determinant of consumption is any recognition of the importance of innovation and technological change. They are credited with no influence on possible consumption choices, nor on the basic drive for betterment or the means of acquiring a higher standard of living. It is said that the introduction of new products has not increased consumption expenditures, and the conclusion is based on an examination of savings, income per consuming unit (roughly a family), and expenditures on consumer durable goods since the year 1900.

It can be shown, however, that innovations have influenced consumption expenditure in other ways than by the introduction of new consumer durables. Important innovations have occurred in other types of products, with a cumulative effect upon consumption and demand.

Progress in a Series of Steps

In defining new products, a distinction is very often made between those which introduce a new range of activities—the automobile, television—and those which improve old activities—labor-saving machinery of all kinds. Deusenberry divides the latter type further into those involving increased expense and those involving decreased expense. Because most of the new household appliances are essentially substitutes for maids, he concludes, it is unlikely that expenditures were increased as these new products appeared, since the incomes would otherwise have been devoted to maid service.

Granted that in the absence of vacuum cleaners and washing machines a larger demand for servants would exist, the automatic devices are not simply and wholly a substitute for maids. Perhaps most important, they are not in the same price range. Simply because the consumer at low levels of income could not afford maid service, mechanical devices may be thought to introduce a new range of activities. It is only to consumers at higher levels of income, where expenditure on maid service takes place, that these appliances may be considered improved methods of performing old activities. The distinction, for purposes of analysing consumption expenditures, is therefore of little value.

What is significant is the fact that the mechanical devices offer a substitute for part of the services of a maid or that each offers a limited range of new activities. Thus consumption expenditure is enabled to increase more gradually and persistently as incomes gradually increase. A small increase in income, insufficient to provide maid service, may be used to purchase a vacuum cleaner or a washing-machine. Since most machinery operates on the principle of the division of labor, it is necessary to add many different machines to provide a complete replacement of existing hand methods. The new products introduced, therefore, have greatly increased the number of items to be ranked in defining a higher standard of living. Progress from one living standard to another may take place in a series of steps of additional consumption expenditure, any one or several of which may be smaller than one considerable shift like that from no maid service to a household servant.

In this connection, innovations in the field of consumer credit have widened the gap between purchasing a home appliance and hiring a maid. The use of installment payments "fractionalizes" the total price paid, and the system has undoubtedly been responsible for the widespread adoption of consumer durables as they are introduced.

Significance of Innovation Itself

But it is doubtful whether innovation should be defined predominantly in terms of the automobile and labor-saving household appliances, striking as these developments have been. In its bearing upon consumption expenditure, the introduction of innovation itself as a recognized part of most of the products which consumers buy is probably more significant.

By convention, consumption expenditures are divided into broad categories of expenditures on food (including drink and tobacco), clothing, households and household operation, furnishings, transportation, amusement, and education. The consumer durable goods which Deusenberry takes as the epitome of innovation are therefore only a small part of consumption expenditure on household operation and on transportation. But innovations have taken place within each of the broad categories, with recognizable effect upon living standards as a whole.

One of the most interesting changes is that in food consumption. Expenditures on food (excluding that consumed on the premises) amounted in 1929 to 18 per cent of personal disposable income, in 1939 to 20 per cent, and in 1950 to 22 per cent, with estimates for later years ranging up to 26 per cent. Most of this increase represents innovation in food processing and marketing, as do the shifts in the composition of the diet. The larger quantities of dairy products, fresh fruits and vegetables purchased stem, of course, from improved refrigeration and transportation techniques. Prepared mixes, pre-packaged meats, frozen juices and baby foods resemble consumer durables in that they are labor-saving.

But again, the innovations have greatly increased the number and variety of consumers' choices, putting the ranking of goods and the progress of improvement in a series of small steps. And packaged cake mixes may lead to increased expenditures where electric mixers do not, precisely because the first may be consumed by families whose incomes are too low to permit purchase of the second.

In the field of clothing, wholly new fabrics have been introduced, as well as altered methods of manufacture and distribution. One result has been to make style, and the necessary changes in style, an important part of the product at every price level. Another result has been to allow more specialized garments to be bought; in other words, to provide a greater number of items, so that clothing expenditure can also increase by small steps as income increases.

Innovations in amusement over the past fifty years include not only the moving-picture, radio, and television, but the growing popularity of various types of sport. The adoption of skiing as a new pastime inevitably increases the demand for ski clothes and equipment, and the automobile induces consumption expenditure in many fields—vacationing and purchased meals being the obvious ones. Innovations in household furnishings include not only the mechanical devices mentioned above, but multi-purpose goods such as chairs and sofas which are also beds, sewing machines which are also tables, and rooms which furnish both dining and living space, or the development of outdoor space with playground or barbecue equipment. The disappearance in household operation of the large pantry or storeroom reflects innovations both in food and in transportation besides representing a change in consumption expenditure.

Consumer Demand for Something New

Such innovations have provided a greater number and variety of consumers' goods of all kinds with a great expansion in the list of goods to be ranked in order of preference. They have also made innovation a familiar part of the standard of living at every level, and a part of nearly every consumption good. Manufacturers have been steadily changing their products. As a result, consumers expect today, when they make a purchase, to buy something recognizably different from the product which they would have secured ten years before. Change is, therefore, a part of the product; it is demanded by consumers and supplied by producers.

This situation does not entirely reflect true technological improvements. If we define a product in terms of its functions and of its performance of those functions, we can recognize changes, for example, in the performance of automobiles over the past twenty years, but little change in their functions. On the other hand, the introduction of synthetic textiles has provided fabrics with new functions (or characteristics) whose performance has steadily improved. Both of these changes may be termed technological. They are, in the main, the result of competition via innovation, and they include steady and gradual improvement in a well-known product as well as wholly new products, which appear less frequently.

Other types of product change serve no technical purpose. Changes in design or styling, or product differentiation by advertising and trademark, are of interest to the theory of monopolistic competition as attempts by the producer to secure a special market for his special good. But such changes are also important to consumption, for such products are purchased partly because they satisfy the demand for change and something new. Packaging, names, slogans, and design serve to identify today's household soap or toothbrush just as an automatic shift or power steering identifies the late-model automobile.

Simply because so many technical improvements have occurred, it is possible to associate change *per se* with technical improvements, and to take any product change as one for the better.[1] In many markets, such product changes are more significant than price changes, and competition among producers occurs with the development and introduction of technically improved and modified products. The consumer's appetite for change is thus both satisfied and continually whetted by the insistence that

[1]This association of change with technical improvement is generally abetted by advertising policy. The research and development efforts of individual companies are publicized not only to promote good public relations but also simply to advertise the product (which may or may not have been a part of the company's research program). Furthermore, what may be called pseudo-scientific or technical changes are very often claimed by advertisements extolling a "secret ingredient" or "new development" in a familiar product.

change has in fact taken place, that this year's model is new and different (and therefore better).

Conclusions

The implications of this brief discussion are various. The introduction of new and modified products, tending to make innovation a part of the American standard of living, has been an important cause of the drive to a higher standard of living. Innovation itself, having become familiar and being associated with technical improvements, is now demanded by consumers and sold by producers. In ranking products in the order of their superiority, consumers give weight to the innovations involved, which may be technical or non-technical.

The drive to a higher standard of living is, therefore, partly a drive to more innovation and novelty, as new products have become available and changed products are increasingly common. Secondly, innovations have greatly extended the number of different types of consumers' goods available, and in many cases have made possible an increase in consumption expenditure by a series of small steps.

Finally, once innovation is understood to include modifications or changes in the product as well as wholly new products, it is practically impossible to measure, statistically, any increase in consumption expenditure which may have occurred. During the World War II controversy over the validity of the Bureau of Labor Statistics price index, downgrading in terms of quality and scarcity of products became vividly apparent. The continuous upgrading and modification, in terms of quality and availability of products, have not, perhaps, been sufficiently emphasized.

The temptation to dwell upon the years after 1900 as the era of two new industries, automobiles and radio, should not prevent the realization that innovations have taken place in existing industries with existing products. They are not so obvious because they did not require the establishment of wholly new firms and markets; their cumulative effect on consumption, however, may have been equally important to that of the automobile and radio.

Eleanor Sauer Daniel

SOME OBSERVATIONS ON PERSONAL SAVINGS AND LIFE INSURANCE SAVINGS

Surely, it must have been the subject of this essay which provoked the observation that:

> Economists disagree not only about the future but also about the past. Many historical events are given different and contradictory explanations. It is in this respect that economists are even worse than physicians. Physicians, when they do not act in concert, may disagree on the therapy, the prognosis and the diagnosis, but as pathologists they usually agree on the post-mortem, though perhaps only because the dead cannot well go to another pathologist. Economists normally remain in disagreement on post-mortems.[1]

In almost no other field of economic interest is understanding so limited as for the savings and investment process. Yet there are excuses for the deficiency. Not only are there major gaps in the statistics, but the entire process is so complex that it almost defies synthesis of what is already known. Under the circumstances economists cannot be blamed if they retreat into the refuge of broad generalities or protective technicalities.

This essay, unfortunately, may only add to the brew. It presents no reasoned thesis, but a series of random observations which point to the humble conclusion that a fresh approach is called for, perhaps under the aegis of the "money-flow" concepts that have been in process of development over the last decade. Much of the present difficulty may stem from the attempt to force unlike situations into a mechanistic "savings" and "investment" mold which in no way reflects the forces shaping developments in the real world.

---

[1] Fritz Machlup, "Do Economists Know Anything?", *American Scholar*, Spring 1953.

Personal savings are a main focus of many of today's most significant economic problems. To list only a few questions on which the behavior of savings is believed to have a bearing: There are those who contend that, over the long run, the country may choke on an oversupply of savings. This rests on the presumed tendency of saving to rise in relation to income as incomes rise. (This view has recently lost some of its popularity, but cannot yet be relegated to the potter's field of defunct economic theories.) On the other hand, there is an opposite theory that a long run insufficiency of saving may shackle the investment which underlies rising standards of living. Among the villains in this piece are the levelling down of income distribution and dampening tax influences. If the economy survives passage between Scylla and Charybdis, it may yet founder on the fears of those who see a growing concentration of personal savings in the hands of financial intermediaries. Among other consequences, this tendency is believed hostile to the dynamic forces inherent in new and small businesses.

In the shorter run, encouragement of savings, and certain preferred uses of saving to combat inflation, have been in the forefront of economic discussion for a major portion of the last decade. Currently (February 1954), the consumer, and his intentions with respect to the use both of his current income and of his accumulated "past savings," are the crucial uncertainties in the minds of economic forecasters and planners.

Possible Influence of Personal Savings

The importance of personal saving does not stem from its quantitative significance. In prosperous peacetime years it has accounted for only five per cent to eight per cent of incomes after taxes, and much less in time of depression. The proportion as a claim against total output is lower still.

Rather, weight is attached to personal saving either because it is considered to exert a dynamic influence on consumption, investment and related factors, or because it is regarded as a pulse measuring changes occurring in such areas. Over the years the theoretical interpretation of the saving process has fluctuated roughly between two poles: (1) the belief that the decision to save is an autonomous one consciously made by individuals under the stimulus of various motivating factors and (2) that certainly from the standpoint of the economic community as a whole, and perhaps for most individuals also, it is purely a residual, representing the difference between changes in income (largely uncontrollable from the individual standpoint) and consumption decisions.

The pendulum is now swinging back to a more balanced realization that personal savings as defined currently are a resultant of both types of forces, with some components more largely dependent on conscious decision than others.

Forms of Personal Savings

Definition of terms is essential in any discussion of personal savings because the current concept permits of so many variations. Purely for statistical convenience, this discussion will proceed in terms of Department of Commerce definitions for total personal savings and, for life insurance savings, an independent estimate roughly comparable in concept.

Strictly speaking, "personal savings" is a misnomer for the Commerce data which include all private noncorporate savings. The hodge-podge thus encompasses forms of savings motivated by business as well as personal considerations, varying in liquidity, in the degree to which conscious decisions are involved, in the type of agency administering their disposition. These components behave very differently; they do not move together over time, either long period or shorter cycle. The make-up of this savings aggregate can be categorized in different ways. From one view point the savings total comprises at least three different forms:

1. *Contractual saving,* such as life insurance payments and contributions to pension funds, is the stable "hard core." Closely related in nature is saving by repayment of consumer and mortgage debt. Debt contraction and repayment, however, varies more widely from business peaks to troughs, and in the case of home mortgage debt, is also considerably influenced by the swings of the longer building cycle.
2. Individuals also save in the more or less *liquid forms* of bank deposits, savings and loan shares, government and private securities, and currency. Such savings are more erratic. These tend to be used as a kind of revolving fund—to purchase durable goods, meet emergencies, or meet commitments to maintain contractual savings.
3. Individuals invest some savings directly in homes and farms. Furthermore, since in real life people do not always separate their business transactions from their personal affairs, reported *"direct personal savings"* also include invest-

ments in unincorporated businesses, including highly volatile business inventories. This muddies any relationship of personal savings to general economic conditions. An increase in personal savings could, on the one hand, be an evidence of prosperity, or it could evidence the piling up of unsaleable goods. Similarly, the idea that a drop in saving cushions the effect of falling income on consumer expenditure is open to question. The drop may be centered in direct investment. Such investment is at least as dynamic in promoting greater business activity as are consumer expenditures. Thus the net cushioning effect of a drop in savings for general business may be greatly overstated by this kind of calculation.

Another point must also be kept in mind. Since "personal savings" represent the differences between individuals' income after taxes ("disposable income") and their expenditures, it is a *net* figure in which the savings made by some people are offset by the "dissavings" of those living beyond their incomes, and financing their excess expenditures by borrowing or drawing down previously accumulated assets. Indeed, the same family will often save in one form and at the same time draw down other assets or incur additional debt. Thus the net savings figure is, in all probability, only a small fraction of the gross amounts saved by individuals. It represents merely the net outcome of many conflicting tendencies and, as such, is a poor barometer of what is actually occurring in the economy.

Short Term Volatility—Long Term Stability

Personal savings are extremely volatile. During the past twenty-five years the proportion of income saved at trough years of business recessions has characteristically been less than at the preceding peak. These ratios have swung more violently in some cycles than others. Furthermore, the proportion of disposable income saved at comparable levels of business activity —peak to peak and trough to trough—has varied widely. The current ratio (7.5 per cent) is historically high, even for boom years. However, series compiled by reputable authorities for even longer periods in general find no definite secular trend in the savings ratio. This finding of stability, so far at least, thus confounds those who are haunted by the spectre of either too much or too little savings.

Within this total, however, there do seem to be persistent changes in the composition of saving which make its overall stability all the more surprising. At least to this observer, they seem much more significant from the standpoint of comprehending economic process than any accidental trend or lack of it in the non-homogeneous aggregate we choose to call "savings." Of particular interest is the tendency (how pronounced is a matter of debate) for contractual savings and savings through financial intermediaries to increase in relative importance over the long span.

Factors Underlying Life Insurance Savings

Life insurance savings are of sufficient importance within the contractual and institutional sector to justify some observations on their behavior and the factors underlying it. At the very least they illustrate the complexities introduced in the channels by which funds move from individual saver to ultimate investor when both elaborate contractual decisions and financial intermediaries are involved. This discussion will be directed to the savings end of the process, since the implications for investment have recently been spelled out in an excellent paper by Dr. James J. O'Leary.[2]

Savings through life insurance currently account for some 25-30 per cent of all personal savings in the United States. Life insurance savings are defined here as the yearly increase in assets, excluding any increases resulting from capital gains or company borrowing rather than income. They also exclude any increase in capital stock, which is not regarded as personal saving governed by usual life insurance motives. From this total is subtracted any net increase in policyholder borrowing, since such policy loans represent "dissaving" by some policyholders.

The chief characteristic of life insurance savings is their stability. Unlike both direct and liquid forms of saving, life insurance savings are maintained in good years and bad. They remained positive even when all other forms of saving were dissipated on balance in 1932-1934, and they represented 166 per cent of the low figure to which all net savings plummeted in 1938.

[2]"The Institutional Saving-Investment Process and Current Economic Theory," presented before the American Economic Association, December 28, 1953. Dr. O'Leary notes that institutional investors cannot be forced into the mold of liquidity preference theory which is framed in terms of individual investors. The stability of life company savings means that investments are made with a view to keeping fully invested over the long run, rather than on any interest rate expectations or trading approach.

The fact that life insurance savings have been less subject to dissipation during adverse business conditions is one reason why life insurance assets (i.e., *accumulated* savings) have outstripped even many other institutional media (chiefly time and savings deposits and savings and loan assets) in growth since 1929. Added to this, a long run tendency now seems to be emerging for a larger proportion of current income to be devoted to savings in life insurance even in years of comparable business activity. This would obviously accelerate asset accumulation.

Even these limited generalizations do not, however, apply uniformly to the elements which go to make up life insurance savings. Savings through life insurance are merely the net result of amounts *saved* on the one hand through premiums and retention of investment income, and *dissaved* on the other through payment of benefits, dividends, surrenders, and policy loan borrowing, to mention only the major categories. These various gross flows of savings and dissavings are traceable to very different groups in the population. People who pay premiums differ in age, marital, income and occupation status from those who receive benefits. Borrowers are a differently constituted group again. A welter of different motives stands behind each operation.

Naturally, in view of these divergent influences, the various elements do not move together, either cyclically or over the long run. However, where they do show any influence of the changing economic environment, the relationship to income is much more regular than the relationship to the erratic personal savings figures. This regularity lends support to the belief that individuals generally regard life insurance savings more as a necessary expenditure than they do some other forms of saving. The argument that savings are essentially determined as a passive residual of income and expenditure does not apply to the positive side of life insurance saving where conscious savings decisions normally are involved. For dissaving, this view might provide a more convincing interpretation; consumption desires undoubtedly influence some policy loan borrowers, and also influence decisions whether to leave dividends and benefits with the companies or to withdraw them.

Past Behavior of Life Insurance Saving: Income

Income, particularly premium income, has displayed steady long-term growth, retreating in only two of the past twenty-five years (1932-1933). In the 1938 depression total income continued to advance, and in 1949 only a slight diminution of the rate of growth marked the impact of the recession.

The premiums he pays undoubtedly are what the man on the street regards as his savings. Even though these payments cover protection and operating expenses as well as true savings, it is highly unlikely that many mortals think in such sophisticated accounting terms as the economists' definition of savings. Premiums paid in any one year reflect both the decisions to buy insurance made contemporaneously ("new" premiums) and also the cumulative effect of decisions made in earlier years ("renewal" premiums). Quantitatively the latter far outweigh the former: in 1950 new premiums amounted to $0.8 billions, renewal to $6.4 billions. (These figures exclude accident and health premiums; 1950 is the latest year for which a breakdown of new and renewal premiums is obtainable.)

As might be expected from their nature, new and renewal premiums behave somewhat differently when personal income changes. Once individuals have undertaken a commitment to pay premiums, they apparently will go to considerable lengths to meet it. Only in the two worst years of the 'thirties, 1932-1933, did renewal premium payments actually drop below the preceding year's figure. New premiums swing much more readily, however; they declined in ten of the last twenty-five years. As a result of their greater inertia renewal premiums tend to increase as a proportion of income from the peak to the trough of the cycle. New premiums have tended to be geared a little more closely to income; i.e., to represent a more stable proportion.

Implicit in this movement of premiums is a tendency of new life insurance sales to move in accord with disposable income, with ordinary and industrial business showing relatively more stability in the face of business declines than group, which is tied more directly to employment conditions. In 1949, however, with only a slight levelling down of incomes, group business showed itself about as recession-proof as ordinary, bolstered by the strong underlying upsurge in this type of coverage which has prevailed since the War. Investigations covering a slightly longer period, the five cycles from 1921 through 1946, indicate that new ordinary sales may tend to turn down later than general business and to turn up earlier as well. Group sales seem to respond more promptly to a changing economic picture. These patterns are cited because they illustrate the many cross-currents submerged in the flow of savings into life companies.

The other major component of positive life insurance saving is *investment income* earned on accumulated policyholder funds. In 1950, investment and miscellaneous income was $3.1 billions. A large portion of this is reinvested to maintain policy reserves, or build up surplus. Thus, in contrast to premium income, much investment income becomes savings without conscious decision of the policyholder.

Over the twenty-five years, regular premium income and investment earnings have both shown a declining tendency in relation to individuals' income after taxes. Nonetheless, as noted earlier, *net* life insurance saving has tended to move up in relation to income. This has resulted (on the positive side) from the phenomenal growth of accident and health business and miscellaneous income, which has compensated for the relative lag in other premiums. On the "dissaving" side, withdrawals have tended to decrease in relation to personal incomes in even more pronounced fashion than premiums. Thus the increase in net savings has been aided curiously by a growing spread between the uneven relative declines of significant items of income and outgo.

Behavior of Insurance Withdrawals

Policy loans declined steadily during half of the period (1933-1946), and the postwar increase in policyholder borrowing has been negligible when compared with the inflow of new savings into life insurance. Actually, of course, we have no good measure of policyholders' dilution of their life insurance savings through borrowing, since resort is also had to bank loans. These probably explain some of the decline in relative importance of life company policy loans, and also account for the failure of such borrowing to show any perceptible cyclical pattern.

Benefit payments generally, excluding surrender payments, have shown a persistent increase similar to that of premiums. The rate of growth, however, seems to have been slightly lower, reflecting a relative restriction on both death benefits and dividends to policyholders. These are complex totals about which generalization is dangerous. Under the level premium system of insurance, benefits would be expected in any case to lag behind premiums as long as business is growing, and new business has more than doubled since World War II. The unusually favorable mortality trend of recent years further tends to limit the extent of death benefits.

The changing composition of dividends is also an elaborate mixture of conflicting trends. Higher mortality gains operate to increase dividends, but lower excess interest earnings, greater retention of earnings to strengthen reserves and, more recently, some tendency of mutual companies to lower gross premiums, and of excess expense margins to be squeezed by rising costs, work in the opposite direction.

Not only have benefit payments been restricted, but policyholders and beneficiaries have recently chosen to leave more of these amounts with the companies than in some earlier years. In 1952, only one-fifth of all dividends were taken in cash, the rest being used to pay premiums or buy additional insurance, or left at interest. Similarly, 30 per cent of the eligible death benefits, matured endowments and cash surrender values were left to provide income, as against an estimated 10 per cent at the turn of the 'thirties.

Cyclical changes in benefit payments undoubtedly are equally complex, but for the naked eye steady growth has masked any cyclical pattern. Only in 1932-1934 was a decrease in policy dividends sufficient to cause some slight tapering off in total payments. Nor do any of the individual categories of payments, with the possible exception of death benefits, which increased in 1931-1932 and then receded again, show any obvious cyclical pattern. Disability payments are known to exhibit some cyclical variations, but in the general statistics they are lumped with annuity payments, so any fluctuations are disguised.

Policyholder dissaving through *surrenders,* like policy loans, has declined sharply, whether considered in relation to accumulated savings available for withdrawal or to the gross inflow of new savings. This is the component of life insurance saving most clearly sensitive to changing business conditions. Surrender values paid out tripled from 1929 to 1932, jumped 15 per cent from 1937 to 1938 and 25 per cent from 1948 to 1949. (They had been rising ever since the very low war-time levels reached in 1944 but this represented an acceleration of the previous increase.)

The companies' *management expenses and other disbursements* show a definite long-term trend upward, influenced, among other considerations, by price and wage inflation, and by the post-war rise in new business. These expenditures showed some very slight tendency to fall in 1932 and 1938. However, this category is such a catchall that any tendency to vary with business conditions inevitably is blurred.

The upshot of these divergent movements within the life insurance savings total has been that the cyclically more stable elements have tended to outweigh the less stable, producing the persistent growth trend noted earlier. To recapitulate, then, the increase in the long run importance of *accumulated* life insurance savings has resulted from (1) this greater stability in comparison with other forms of personal savings and (2) the tendency of net life insurance savings to increase even in relation to the current flow of income and perhaps (though less clearly) in relation to total personal savings as well.

Past Trends No Guarantee of Future

There are those who, concerned about these growing accretions of funds, and unimpressed by the old saw about trees not growing to the sky, project these trends indefinitely into the future. Such projection, particularly in view of our limited understanding of the tangled underlying forces at work, does not seem warranted. To cite only a few of the elements of uncertainty: how can we assess the effects on future growth of the basic change which appears to have occurred in the position of private life insurance since 1940? While individuals have devoted a fairly constant proportion of increasing income to total security expenditures since 1929, life insurance companies have failed to share in these increasing expenditures except through accident and health premiums. A larger share has gone to government insurance, retirement and pension funds, hospital and medical services. These changes may evidence not only an alteration in the relative importance of different income and occupation groups in the total market but also a changed attitude toward the relative importance of different kinds of coverage. Either could affect both the long run inflow of premium income and also its stability in any future recession.

Similarly, the outflow of funds from the companies might well be stepped up as mortality improvement slackens, as the insured population ages, and as the economy emerges from the flood of liquidity which has submerged both the policy loan and surrender accounts.

These considerations all signal caution in generalizing about the future of life insurance saving. If this be true, how much more should caution be indicated when dealing with the total of which life insurance saving is but one of many variegated parts!

Janet M. Hooks

WOMEN IN THE PROFESSIONS 1870 - 1950

Historians of economic thought usually begin their discourses with "Ancient Times." This enables them to evaluate the contribution to economic analysis of the Greek philosophers, who are credited with laying the basis for much of later economics. Thus economics may be placed on as firm a foundation as other sciences, which also date from the speculations of antiquity.

One of the economic subjects discussed by Plato is the division of labor, concerning which two points are made: that "all things are produced more plentifully and easily, and of a better quality, when one man does one thing which is natural to him and does it at the right time, and leaves other things"; and that there are "diversities of natures among us which are adapted to different occupations."

In almost every culture that we know about, a fundamental basis for the division of labor is the sex of the worker. The work performed by men and by women is not, however, the same from one culture to another. Instead, the very jobs reserved to men in one society may be those which only women do in another.

The prestige connected with the various occupations of any society differs from one culture to another and also is related to the sex of the individual performing the work. Dr. Margaret Mead points out that "Men may cook, or weave or dress dolls or hunt humming-birds, but if such activities are appropriate occupations of men, then the whole society, men and women alike, votes them as important."

In the American economy the general pattern has been that practically all men enter gainful employment. Women, by and large, have traditionally performed unpaid work for their families in the home. Over the years, however, that tradition has been breaking down and an increasing proportion of women have entered the labor market to work for pay.

The first official published census data for women's occupations refer to 1870, when the Industrial Revolution may be said to have been fairly well completed in the United States. At that time there were less than two million women in gainful work and they constituted less than one-seventh of all women of working age. Eighty years later, the 1950 census reported 16 million women in the labor force, and they were nearly 30 per cent of all women in the population fourteen years old and over.

"Prestige" Occupations

The fact of increasing participation by women in paid work is usually taken as one item of evidence as to the high and advancing status which women hold in American culture. The growing industrialization of the United States has resulted in an economy in which families earn money to buy the essentials and comforts of life, rather than "making" a living by providing their own food, clothing and shelter within each family unit. The successful person in our pecuniary society is he who is able to command a large money income. Not only money-making, but working in those particular occupations in which it is possible to obtain large monetary returns, consequently tends to be highly regarded.

Yet, strangely enough, there are some less remunerative occupations which are accorded greater respect than better-paying ones. The President's Commission on Higher Education reported the ranking of ninety occupations by a public opinion poll, from U. S. Supreme Court Justice and physician in the first two places to shoe shiner in the ninetieth. Ranked equal with "member of the board of directors of a large corporation" were architect, chemist, dentist, lawyer, nuclear physicist, priest. Ranked just above or almost equal with "owner of factory that employs about 100 people" were airline pilot, artist who paints pictures that are exhibited in galleries, sociologist, accountant for a large business, biologist, and musician in a symphony orchestra. The factory owner and the member of the board undoubtedly are thought of as making more money than persons in the other occupations of similar prestige. The others receive their elevated position on the occupational ladder in large part by virtue of the fact that they are "professional." In an assessment of the economic status of women, therefore, we may consider advancement in the professional fields as one of the indexes of the occupational progress of women.

The 1950 census shows that 1,964,000, or nearly 12 per cent of all women in the experienced labor force, were in occupations classified as "professional, technical, and kindred." These figures contrast with the less than 94,000 women of the 1870 census who can be traced to roughly comparable occupations, and who were less than five per cent of all women workers of that date.

The trend has been not only of increasing participation by women in professional work, but of growing variety in the types of professional work they do. Eighty-odd years ago, 90 per cent of the women in professional occupations were teachers or college presidents, professors and instructors; another six per cent were musicians and music teachers; one per cent were nurses. Thus all the other professional fields together constituted insignificant opportunities for women in this stratum of work. By 1950, women teachers were far more numerous but had dropped to 44 per cent of all women professional and technical workers. (Teachers here include college presidents, professors and instructors for comparability.) Trained nurses (including students) were 24 per cent of the total. Each of nine other occupations had one to five per cent—specifically, accountants and auditors, artists and art teachers, dietitians and nutritionists, editors and reporters, librarians, musicians and music teachers, religious workers, social and welfare workers (except group), and medical and dental technicians. Nearly 12 per cent were in still other varied types of professional work.

Impact of a Major War

Because of changes in the 1950 census procedures, revisions of earlier data will be necessary before detailed comparisons for individual occupations in 1950 and in former periods can be made. We do have, however, comparable data for 1870 to 1940, and 1940 census data for the experienced labor force can be adjusted so as to be approximately comparable with that for 1950. It is possible, therefore, to see whether the changes from 1940 to 1950 tend to continue known earlier trends in professional work for women.

This recent ten-year period — an era of a major conflict—can be considered as exhibiting in concentrated form many of the forces active in a less dramatic fashion at other times. Wars have an important impact on women's occupations, because they draw women into new fields of work, in some of which they continue afterwards. War periods also tend to speed up or change the direction of other factors in occupational trends. Because of overriding necessity, concepts of the traditional sphere of women have less weight in allocating jobs to workers. Public policy attempts in a positive way to shape industry and employment to the nation's needs. Technology, always important in the rise and fall of fields of work, in wartime is consciously adjusted to a limited labor force in ways that affect women's work. Customary occupational barriers are given up, even though reluctantly, to advance the war effort. Furthermore, the pressure for maximum production calls forth a boom situation, which opens new opportunities and may reverse trends related to a lower phase of the business cycle.

A brief survey of selected fields of professional work for women, grouped so that trends before 1940 can be referred to, illustrates the relation of changes in occupations to these and other less spectacular influences.

The Teaching Field

Women in teaching at other than the college level numbered 839,836 in 1950. This field consequently offers in sheer numbers a great opportunity to women for employment in professional work.

In its growth, teaching has been outdistanced by others of the professional occupations. But for many decades numbers of women teachers increased at a more rapid rate than the woman labor force as a whole. This appears to have been the result of the simultaneous development of need for teachers in the school system and the availability of growing numbers of women with appropriate training. Such conditions date from about the middle of the nineteenth century, when female seminaries and normal schools were developing, and when compulsory school legislation made its first appearance. The draining off of men for the Civil War in the formative period of the public school system gave an impetus to the employment of women teachers and is believed to have established the pattern.

The period of rapid expansion for women teachers appears to have ended, however, with the Great Depression. The latest census interval brought only a small relative increase in numbers of women teachers (five per cent), following a decline between 1930 and 1940. A decade in which scarcity of jobs limited growth was followed by one in which supply lagged behind needs because of the relative unattractiveness of teaching. The proportion of women among total teachers likewise seems to have stabilized. About three-fourths of all non-college-level teachers were women in both 1950 and 1940, a somewhat smaller ratio than at previous censuses.

Among college presidents, professors and instructors, on the other hand, women continued to be in the minority in 1950, and in fact their proportion dropped from 27 per cent in 1940 to 23 per cent in 1950. Though their numbers rose by over 9,000 in the decade, reaching 29,183 according to the 1950 census, numbers of men grew still more rapidly. The extensive program of veterans' education led to a considerable expansion of educational opportunities for men, and undoubtedly served to increase the employment of men on instructional staffs at these advanced levels.

Relative to general teaching, occupations at the collegiate level have been of minor significance for women, but there has been a sustained relative growth, which continued in 1940-50. In 1940 there was only one woman college president, professor, or instructor for each forty in general teaching. By 1950 the ratio had become one to twenty-nine.

Trained Nurses

World War II brought tremendously increased demands for nurses and greatly improved standards of pay and conditions of employment. The 468,994 trained professional nurses and student nurses reported by the 1950 census represented a rate of increase over 1940 of 30 per cent, about the same as that of the woman labor force as a whole.

The establishment of nursing as a profession had already been well completed. Its beginnings date from the Civil War, when the work of the U. S. Sanitary Commission not only led many women to give their services as nurses during the emergency, but also resulted in standards and training procedures appropriate to an expanding professional field. The rise of the professional nurse accompanied the transfer of care of the sick from home to hospital and the expansion of the public health services.

The impact of public policy and of social change was felt prior to World War II in the nursing profession. From 1940 to

1950, however, the war situation added over 100,000 women to this field, the largest increment in any professional occupation. In 1950, as in 1940, about 98 per cent of all trained nurses (including students) were women. Recent evolution of the field has brought specialized work approaching in skill that of the doctor himself.

Social, Welfare and Religious Workers

A hundred years ago enlightened opinion held that little could be done toward solving problems of poverty. The accepted view was that charitable assistance should be given for the spiritual benefit of the giver as much as for the material assistance of the recipient, but that care should be taken not to misdirect help to the undeserving. With the growth of urban life, and the almost complete dependence on money earnings for a living, situations became increasingly common in which, even though "deserving," the family in distress could not get help from relatives, fellow church members, or neighbors.

Like nursing and the teaching of children, so also aid to the poor or distressed was a traditional sphere for women in the home. So, too, as social work left the home, developed professional standards, and became a recognized field of work, numbers of women in this employment increased. By 1950 there were 59,913 women social and welfare (including recreation and group) workers. Women were, as in 1940, 64 per cent of the total. Another 28,973 women were religious workers, but they dropped from 76 to 69 per cent of all religious workers.

The rate of growth among women in these two fields together had been considerable up to 1940, the depression decade alone adding some 30,000 women to the combined occupations. In the years from 1940 to 1950, about 12,000 women entered social and welfare work, a rate of growth of 25 per cent. Numbers of women in religious work showed a slight decline. This drop in numbers was more than offset, however, by the numerical increase among women clergymen, an occupation included below with the learned professions.

"Cultural" Occupations

Cultural fields are not thought of as particularly affected by technology. Yet, this has been a major element in trends among women in the entertainment field and in music. The development of the phonograph, motion picture, radio and television have made shifts in the nature and extent of women's employment in these fields.

From 1940 to 1950 the number of women musicians increased by one-fifth, representing the resurgence of a field that had been relatively wanting in vitality since about 1910. Women in entertainment fields (including actresses, athletes, dancers and dancing teachers, entertainers, and sports instructors and officials) rose by 39 per cent. Women artists and art teachers were 41 per cent higher. Recent growth in these three groups of occupations contrasts with declines during the depression period. Fluctuations in the rate of growth in earlier census periods also reflect their particular vulnerability to unfavorable economic conditions.

The expansion of educational opportunities in the past century played a dual role in three other "cultural" occupations. An educated population has provided a market for newspapers, journals, books and libraries. At the same time, the advance in requisite training facilities for women has enabled them to share in resulting vocational opportunities. The number of women reported as librarians, as editors and reporters, and as authors increased from 1940 to 1950 by 44, 84, and 35 per cent respectively. Other data for women in the foregoing occupations are as follows:

	Number of Women	*Per cent of Total*	
	1950	1950	1940
Musicians and music teachers	79,626	49	41
Entertainment fields	35,388	32	32
Artists and art teachers	30,756	38	34
Librarians	49,356	89	90
Editors and reporters	29,289	32	25
Authors	6,235	39	33

The Learned Professions

Entrance to medicine, theology, and the law was attained by women only as the fruit of a long struggle to be allowed the necessary training. As late as 1871 one authority stated: "If females persist in attempting to endure the rigor of hard study, hospitals and asylums must need be erected alongside of colleges for women . . . higher education of females is a mistake full of unreason and fruitful of sorrow." The first woman to receive a medical diploma did so in 1849. The first to graduate from a theological seminary did so in 1851. Legal training was generally obtained by "reading law" in a law office until 1870, so that women were effectively barred until then. In all of these fields women have made progress. Rates of growth from 1940 to 1950 were above that for the woman labor force as a whole, though numbers continued quite small. Data for these fields are as follows:

	Number of Women	*Per cent of Total*	
	1950	1950	1940
Physicians, surgeons and osteopaths	12,575	6	5
Dentists	2,076	3	2
Clergymen	6,847	4	2
Lawyers and judges	6,333	3	2

Scientific and Technical Occupations

The importance of scientists and technicians in modern industrial society was multiplied many times by the war. Wartime increases in several fields reflect the development of training programs for such urgently needed types of workers, government encouragement of employers to utilize women more extensively in work not usual for them, and the desire on the part of women to contribute to the war effort. Increases from 1940 to 1950 in the number of women in some fields of this character were: Laboratory technicians (including testing, medical, and dental), 144 per cent; draftsmen, 455 per cent; chemists, 340 per cent; civil, electrical, and other technical engineers, 647 per cent; and technicians (not elsewhere classified), 355 per cent. Except for laboratory technicians, these nevertheless remained small fields for women, as the following figures show:

	Number of Women	*Per cent of Total*	
	1950	1950	1940
Technicians, laboratory	61,159	39	35
Draftsmen	8,621	7	2
Chemists	7,629	10	3
Engineers, technical	6,652	1	*
Technicians (not elsewhere classified)	4,313	16	9

* Less than 0.5 per cent.

Diversity in Professional Trends

From the foregoing review of trends in some of the professional fields in which women work, several types of occupation may be distinguished according to the position that women hold in them.

In the first group may be included occupations which have arisen as the result of the transfer of activities outside the home and their further development. They have in the past offered rapidly expanding opportunities to women as paid workers. With the completion of the transfer, the rate of growth in the corresponding activities has diminished, but the absolute numbers and proportions of women are large.

In a second group of occupations there are minor but substantial proportions of women. In these fields women have a place in many instances just because of their sex—to take the role of the heroine, to supply the soprano voice in the opera, to write the articles for the woman's page.

In a third group may be placed those occupations which once were virtually closed to women and in which in 1950 women still had only a small part. Though all fields have at least some women, it is only the woman with a strong drive and exceptional ability who enters and remains in occupations in this group. Often, too, she must carve out a unique niche for herself to be successful.

Finally, there are the occupations which have been similar to those just mentioned, but which as a result of the war showed tremendous rates of growth for women. Only the future will determine in which of these the wartime gains made by women will remain.

There is some evidence that the distribution of women in all the various occupations and industries in the economy has been growing more like that of the labor force as a whole. Whether or not this is true within the professional and technical field, there is no doubt that women have had a significant and growing share in this highly-regarded type of activity.

Irma Daum Pratt

INVESTMENT MANAGEMENT: SOME TANGIBLES AND INTANGIBLES

To some individuals, "Wall Street" denotes fabulous profits; to others, who remember October of 1929, it still suggests utter devastation. Neither concept, however, reflects the situation as it is today. The famous street has had a colorful history, to be sure. But the scandals, the huge fortunes amassed and sometimes lost, are almost as much things of the past as trading under the famous Buttonwood Tree. In the present day, "Wall Street" has new significance—that of representing the investment world.

Investment has been defined as the productive employment of capital. This is achieved by the acceptance of a creditor position, through the purchase of bonds and other obligations, or of an ownership position, through the purchase of stocks.

It is doubtful whether there are many individuals who, although they may not be owners of securities themselves, are not dependent in some way on them. Much of the income of life insurance companies derives from investments. Pensions, disability payments, and even strike benefits received by members of labor unions, are supported by or increased through investment income.

Keith Funston, president of the New York Stock Exchange, said recently that "democratic capitalism, the ownership of the means of production by millions of Americans, is one of the most powerful ideas of our time." Individual ownership of common stocks has increased tremendously in recent years. The noteworthy growth of mutual funds is one indication of this. The recent liberalization of many state laws to permit trust officers, savings banks and life insurance companies to invest in common stocks is another.

This increasing dependence on common stocks, doubtless accelerated by inflation and the fear of more inflation, has brought about a marked change in the management of investments. Today, the investment manager is an integral part of the financial field. His responsibilities are weighty. He relies upon study, hard work, the careful use of known and proven tools, and the unemotional evaluation of miscellaneous events and information to form the basis for the exercise of judgment.

The work of individual investment managers covers a wide range of objectives. The goal of a life insurance company is different from that of a savings bank or an eleemosynary institution; all of these differ from the usual objectives of an individual account. Since the subject is a broad one, these remarks refer primarily to the management of security investments for individual owners.

Development of Investment Counseling

Whereas professional management has long been an established department of banks and of life and fire insurance companies, it has grown notably in recent years as applied to individual accounts. The investment complacency of the 1920's, shattered by the stock market crash in 1929, never reasserted itself in its old terms. As never before, institutions and individuals have redoubled their vigilance, in the hope of avoiding similar losses in the future. The protection of professional investment management has come into great demand during the past two or three decades. The term "investment counseling," virtually unknown thirty years ago, has become a standard part of our language.

Establishing Objectives

The preservation of the principal of a fund under supervision is the first responsibility for the investment manager or adviser. Secondly, he must find suitable investments to provide an appropriate income return in the form of interest or dividends. Thirdly, when appropriate, capital appreciation is an important consideration.

The establishment of a long-range program involves consideration of many factors. Family responsibilities are carefully reviewed. Income from work or profession, insurance protection, savings and reserves for emergencies of all kinds, or for education of children, are all taken into account. In short, a program for an individual is tailored to his particular requirements and desires, present and future. Sometimes, too, clients have preferences in regard to industries, or securities, which have a bearing on the program established. Clients have been known to request the omission of securities of the tobacco, liquor, or drug industries. Such views reflect deep personal convictions to which sympathetic attention must be accorded.

The tax status of an individual can, at times, alter to a marked degree the investment manager's selection of securities. If the client is in a tax bracket where additional income would be taxed at a rate over 50 per cent, the investment manager might well consider the purchase of tax-exempt bonds, or investments in special stock situations where all or part of dividend payments is non-taxable as income. To these personal aims and preferences the investment manager must fit the appropriate investment program.

As a basis for good judgment, a variety of aspects of our American system of free enterprise, both tangible and intangible, must be noted and placed in proper perspective. Often these considerations carry greater weight than actual statistical analysis of a security or industry.

General Business Conditions

To carry out his primary responsibility, that of maintaining capital, action may be taken at times to increase the reserve portion of the account (high-grade bonds, cash or equivalent) and to decrease the position in stocks. Conversely, at other times reserves may be decreased and additional common stock bought.

The trend of business is the first, but not the only, consideration. Actually, the stock market in recent years has appeared to be influenced considerably less by current business conditions than in the past. As this is written, for example, business indices have been declining for several months—yet the best-known index of stock prices is reaching new highs almost daily. Time will tell, of course, whether unemployment statistics, industrial production, or the Dow-Jones Industrial Average is the most accurate barometer. In the meantime, the investment manager must try to determine how far-reaching newly developed trends may be.

Indices such as those for national income, gross national product, and industrial production, as reported by the various governmental agencies, provide significant clues concerning the status of business. The pattern of other indices, none of which is independently conclusive, may throw light on a particular industry or group of industries. Among these are production of steel, electric power, crude oil, starts for new homes, department store sales, consumer credit, freight-car loadings, sales of durable goods, and commodity prices. Often one segment of the economy enjoys prosperity while another is suffering its own private recession, as did the textile industry, for example, from 1948 to 1952. Unemployment figures are watched carefully in Wall Street as well as in Washington.

Survey of the Money Market

Since high-grade bonds as a rule move with the trend in interest rates, a study of the forces in operation in the money market must not be overlooked in the management of investments. The Federal Reserve open-market operations, changing of reserve requirements, the re-discount rate, credit policy, and even informal directives to member banks, can exert a powerful influence. The Treasury's refunding policies and the type of securities offered for sale are also significant. These policies of the monetary authorities are frequently changed in the light of prevailing business conditions; an interpretation of the actions of the Federal Reserve and Treasury may provide important indications helpful to the investment manager.

Impact of Unforeseen Events

Probably no other group is more vitally concerned with world affairs than those charged with the responsibilities for investments. Important events, social and political, must be weighed and discounted. For example, in the early summer of 1950, when the North Korean armies marched across the 38th parallel, the boom which occurred during and following World War II had all but spent itself. A readjustment in business conditions was due. The sudden outbreak of war forced an immediate re-evaluation of further expectations. After the initial jolt to our economy, an entirely new set of forces developed. Government expenditures increased sharply and the public, determined not to be without cars, electric appliances, sheets, sugar and other consumers' items, went on a buying spree. This was accompanied by further shrinkage in the purchasing power of the dollar. By January of 1951, the Bureau of Labor Statistics index of wholesale prices had surpassed the highs established following World War II.

Unforeseen events, devastating as they may be, certainly test the investment manager's perception, judgment and agility. Decisions, at times, must be reversed in a matter of hours. However, the investment manager must also be aware that the ultimate effect of unforeseen events may be quite different from what is first expected and guard his conclusions accordingly.

Dynamics of the Economy

History through the ages has recorded the rise and fall of many nations, brought about at least in part by economic factors. It is important to the investment manager to know whether the American system of free enterprise has reached stagnation. Geographical barriers have been pushed back. Competition from other quarters of the world is increasing. On the other hand, since 1940 there has been a tremendous upsurge in population with the accompanying needs for additional dwellings, goods and services. It has been reported that almost four million babies were born in the United States during 1953. Such expansion provides a dynamic force. But will this rate of growth be maintained in the future?

Our economy has been characterized by a tremendous increase in technological development. Only twenty years ago, there was little thought of air-conditioned homes, jet propulsion, synthetic detergents, nylon and the vast family of synthetic fibres, miracle drugs, television, electronic calculators, automobiles made from plastic reinforced with fibreglass, new light but strong metals, or the use of radioactive isotopes to cure dreaded diseases. The list is endless. One new development leads to others. For example, *The Wall Street Journal* recently reported that the demand for revolving doors, such as those used for public and office buildings, had increased sharply. Architects have found this type of door particularly well suited for use in air-conditioned buildings. Labor works shorter hours than formerly and has more leisure time for sports, thereby increasing the demand for athletic equipment.

Our society is one of constant replacement and substitution. An illustration can be drawn from the change in types of home-heating methods. Coal was for years the primary fuel. With the discovery of and production from vast oil fields, oil became the popular fuel. More recently, with the development of an extensive network of pipelines, natural gas began to be used for this purpose thousands of miles from its source. It is conceivable that atomic energy may step into the forefront in the future. In the past, basic fuels have not completely replaced each other in turn. The results of their domination at various times, however, have had important effects upon the stocks and bonds involved.

The investment manager must be wary, however, in appraising the effects of new products. Research and production expenditures may be too costly to result in a readily marketable item. Here, too, good judgment is important.

Psychological Factors

Abraham Lincoln said in a speech in Ohio in 1859, "Public opinion in this country is everything." The investment manager understands only too well the accuracy of this statement. The diagnosing of public opinion and mass action represents a necessary but nebulous problem he must face.

Too often rules of logic fail to have any value in this phase of study. The Florida real estate "bubble" and the stock market boom and crash in the late 1920's and 1930's are examples of how far mass action can affect established conditions or trends. Some indication of the general public's investment psychology must be made and assayed even though no precise yardstick exists. A high level of optimism may be indicated by large volume of trading in the security markets and newspaper headlines of stock market advances. Enthusiasm of this sort may indicate a dangerous peak. On the other hand, an atmosphere of deep gloom may indicate that a decline has run its course.

The cumulative effect of the public's fear of war, of inflation or deflation, may have considerable influence on the economy and the security markets. It is helpful to note, for example, whether the public in general is saving or dissaving, or whether the demand for consumers' goods is normal or expanded.

Perhaps the most important consideration for an investment manager in this respect is to try to keep his decisions above influence by the extremes in optimism or pessimism. He does not always succeed, but his objectivity generally is greater than that of the individual investor.

Political Considerations

A survey of domestic politics may seem incongruous to the work of investment management. Nevertheless, administrative reports such as President Eisenhower's series of messages on economic affairs, the budget, welfare, agriculture, and housing, merit study because they propose to be blue prints for legislation. Actual enactment does not necessarily follow, of course. The investment manager must not let his own political beliefs or wishful thinking obstruct his appraisal of probabilities or effects of legislation. He should discern, for example, whether the tax structure provides sufficient incentive to business enterprise for expansion. Are various markets free or are they hampered by improper and unnecessary regulations? What steps are being taken to keep the economy of the country in balance if business activity declines? Will governmental policies concerning our place in the world consumers' market prove effective? Whether he personally agrees or disagrees with what is done has no bearing upon the work of the investment manager.

Analysis of Industries and Individual Securities

Investment management requires the technical skill to analyze industries and individual securities. Calculation of numerous ratios, comparison of such items as earnings, sales, asset values of one company with others in the same industry—these are the tools of the trade. They are comparable to a physician's knowledge of anatomy. However, the scope of the work goes far beyond the accurate analysis of balance sheets, income accounts and other historical data as reported in statistical services, prospectuses and annual reports.

Procedures in analysis of various industries cannot be stereotyped. No ironclad rules apply and each analysis must be augmented with a study of particular circumstances or characteristics that may apply. One industry may depend on population trends and another on prices for certain basic commodities. Still others are highly dependent on labor. Accuracy in dealing with facts or figures is the watchword.

In appraising a security, whether it be for purchase, retention, or sale, the estimate of management is an elusive but all-important factor. The securities of more than one corporation have fallen into disfavor as the result of poor management. Managements of our giant corporations are charged with the responsibilities for financing, budgeting, production, planning and control, engineering, research, design, purchasing, marketing and personnel. All these activities must result in public acceptance and return a profit. They must also be related to such external problems as defense needs, taxation and public attitudes.

As in other instances, no exact scientific formula applies in appraising the management of a corporation. The investment manager draws conclusions regarding the success of management, not from the size of the dividend declarations but rather by the efficiency, integrity and ingenuity with which the management operates. Ploughing back the correct proportion of earnings—neither too little nor too much—for further expansion and development; meeting competition in the industry both as to products and prices in a realistic manner; and the handling of unprofitable operations either by correction or abandonment, give indication of the quality of management.

Making the Final Decision

It is against this background of respectful attention to existing facts, both present and past, combined with accurate analyses of securities, industries, and the action of the security markets, that the investment manager decides the price and time at which to buy or sell a security or whether a security already owned should be retained. This is no static existence. Decisions must be re-examined constantly in the light of changing conditions and related to the ultimate goal.

It may seem that the work of the investment manager, both in bulk and complexity, would necessitate his simulating the mythical Janus who reportedly could face in two directions at one time. Such ability would certainly prove helpful. But although surveying the past and looking to the future are important parts of the task, probably even more essential is the view "straight ahead." Sound objectives adapted to prevailing conditions—that is the foundation stone of confident investment management.

The Contributors

Marjorie S. Belcher, 1938 (*Town Finance in Seventeenth Century Plymouth* and *Publication Committee*) has been an economist in the European Program Office of the Mutual Security Agency in Washington since 1952. She received her M.A. from Mount Holyoke in 1940; during World War II she was with the Board of Economic Warfare and directly afterward spent a year and a half in Tokyo on the staff of the Foreign Trade Division of the Economic and Scientific Section of SCAP Headquarters; she subsequently spent four years as assistant to Dr. John R. Steelman.

Carolyn Shaw Bell, 1941 (*Innovation and Consumption*) is a member of the Department of Economics at Wellesley College. She received her Ph.D. in economics from London University in 1949; she was an economist in the Office of Price Administration for several years and has also done economic research for the National Security Resources Board; in 1952-53 she was assistant to the director of research, Insular Marketing Project, Social Science Research Center, University of Puerto Rico. She has written for the *Quarterly Journal of Economics* and *The Annals.*

W. Mary Breed, M.A. 1924 (*Britain's Small Shopkeepers*) was appointed in December, 1953, to a post as clerical officer in the Monopolies and Restrictive Practices Commission, in London. She is a graduate of Girton College, Cambridge University, and has an M.A. from Cambridge as well as from Mount Holyoke. She has worked with various international agencies at Geneva, and in the Geneva and London offices of Aluminium Limited; she entered government service in 1939 and from 1942 through 1953 was in the Consumer Needs Section of the Board of Trade.

Carol Colver, 1934 (*Economic Bases for Power Markets in the Pacific Northwest*) is with a mortgage servicing company in Beverly Hills, California. She received her M.A. in 1935 from the University of Wisconsin; she did economic research for the Federal Deposit Insurance Corporation from 1936 to 1942, when she joined the Bonneville Power Administration and worked on the county surveys described in her article.

Eleanor Sauer Daniel, 1936 (*Some Observations on Personal Savings and Life Insurance Savings*) is Research Associate for the Mutual Life Insurance Company of New York, an organization with which she has been connected since 1940. She received her M.A. from Columbia in 1937; has been research economist for the U. S. Steel Corporation and lecturer in economics at Brooklyn College; she has served on life insurance industry committees and technical committees of the National Bureau of Economic Research; she is the author of *Our National Debt and Our Savings* (with S. Foster and J. J. O'Leary) and has contributed many articles to various professional publications.

Helen F. Demond, 1925 (*Publication Committee*) is Chief, Statistics of Income Branch, Statistics Division, Internal Revenue Service, in Washington. She received her M.A. from Mount Holyoke, where she was instructor in economics from 1927 to 1929; she has also done graduate work at the University of Chicago and at American University. Since 1931 she has worked as an economist and statistician for various agencies and departments of the Federal Government; in 1952 she received a citation from Mount Holyoke College for outstanding Federal Government service.

Marion Hamilton Gillim, 1930 (*Family Allowances in Great Britain*) is Associate Professor of Economics at Barnard College and has a Ph.D. from Columbia University. She has taught at the Owensboro Senior High School in Kentucky and at the New Jersey College for Women, and was a member of the Department of Economics and Sociology at Mount Holyoke from 1942 to 1949. For three years after that she was a Consultant in International Labor Statistics for the U. S. Bureau of Labor Statistics, serving throughout Central and South America (especially Costa Rica, Ecuador, Peru, and Uruguay) as adviser on family expenditure surveys and price indexes.

Ella Tambussi Grasso, 1940 (*Canal Fever: The Development of a Connecticut Valley Town*) is a member of the General Assembly of the State of Connecticut. She was elected to this office in 1952 and serves on the Education and Public Personnel Committees. She is also editor of the *Connecticut Democratic News*. She received her M.A. from Mount Holyoke in 1942 and for several years thereafter was Assistant Director of Research, War Manpower Commission for Connecticut.

Rosemary Danes Hale, 1940 (*Britain's Trade* 1945-1950: *An Example of Socialist Planning*) is a part-time instructor in economics and social science at Lake Forest College, Illinois. She received her M.A. in 1946 from American University, and has worked for the Department of Agriculture and the War Department.

Elinor Harris, 1944 (*Problems of French Tax Reform*) is an economist with the Division of International Finance of the Board of Governors of the Federal Reserve System, in Washington. She received her M.A. in 1945 and her Ph.D. in 1948, both from Radcliffe. She has also worked for the Federal Reserve Bank of Boston.

Janet M. Hooks, 1933 (*Women in the Professions* 1870-1950) is engaged in research work and graduate study at the University of Illinois, where her husband, V. Lewis Bassie, is Professor of Economics. She has done graduate work at Bryn Mawr (M.A. 1934); she worked for the Bureau of Home Economics of the U. S. Department of Agriculture and the Women's Bureau of the U. S. Department of Labor; she has also written extensively on the employment of women in the United States and Great Britain.

Juliet Fisher Kidney, 1934 (*Publication Committee*) is an economist with the U. S. Government, in Washington. She was graduate assistant and instructor in the Department of Economics and Sociology at Mount Holyoke from 1934 to 1943, with the exception of one year spent at Radcliffe, and received her M.A. from Mount Holyoke in 1937. She served as an economist and historian with the O.P.A. for a number of years.

Frances C. Manning, 1925 (*The Crisis in France*) is economic analyst in the General Economics Department of the Standard Oil Company (N. J.). She has also done economic and statistical work for the American Telephone & Telegraph Company, the Guaranty Trust Company, and several investment firms. She did graduate work in economics at Tufts College, where she received her M.A. in 1927.

Louise Pearson Mitchell, 1927 (*Alexander Hamilton as a Lieutenant of Robert Morris*) teaches economics and economic history at Mills College of Education in New York. She received her M.A. from the University of Pennsylvania in 1928; she has been editorial and research assistant on the *Dictionary of American Biography* and for the National Resources Committee, and an instructor in economics at Adelphi College; with her husband, Broadus Mitchell, she is coauthor of *Practical Problems in Economics* and *American Economic History*. Her article was developed from work she is doing with her husband on a full-length biography of Hamilton.

M. Janice Murphy, M.A. 1950 (*Postwar Intra-European Payments Institutions*) is currently an A.A.U.W. Fellow at the Fletcher School of Law and Diplomacy (administered by Tufts College), where she has been preparing her doctoral dissertation on *Britain and the European Payments Union,* 1950-1953. She was graduated from the University of Connecticut in 1948; was graduate assistant with the Department of Economics and Sociology at Mount Holyoke 1948-1950; was Fulbright Fellow at the University of Manchester (England) 1950-1951; and has held a variety of summer positions as a research assistant and economist. She expects to receive her Ph.D. in International Finance in June, 1954.

Janet Brewster Murrow, 1933 (*Adventure in Economics*) is Senior Alumnae Trustee of Mount Holyoke College. She is chairman of the Board of Trustees for Reid Hall and a member of the board of Sydenham Hospital in New York. She lived in England from 1937 to 1946, where her husband, Edward R. Murrow, represented the Columbia Broadcasting System; she worked in London during the war with the U. S. Office of War Information and was head of Bundles for Britain in England.

Irma Daum Pratt, 1935 (*Investment Management: Some Tangibles and Intangibles*) does investment advisory work with the New York firm of Clayton and Wheaton. She has done graduate work at the New York University Graduate School of Business Administration; she did secretarial and statistical work for several years for the Carnegie Foundation Joint Investment Office and for a member of the New York Stock Exchange. Prior to her present position she was assistant to Miss Clara Taylor, on of the first women investment counselors in the country.

Edith Hyslop Sherrard, 1937 (*Economic History Reconsidered*) is Social Studies Associate at the American Association of University Women, in Washington. She prepares study references on current economic and social problems for the Association's local groups. She has an M.A. from Columbia University and has also done graduate work at Bryn Mawr. She has worked in economic research and statistics with the Chase National Bank in New York and the War Production Board in Washington.

Lucile Tomlinson Wessmann, 1933 (Editor) is a financial writer and investment consultant in New York. She was on the editorial staff of *Barron's National Business and Financial Weekly* for ten years and has contributed articles to other financial publications. She serves annually as editor of *Investment Companies* and is the author of *Successful Investing Formulas* (1947) and its successor *Practical Formulas for Successful Investing* (1953).